A sheer adrenaline rush and unabashedly honest, Dorr's memoir unveils a kaleidoscope of emotions many women hold in the lonely places of their hearts.

Mistakes of our past can be celebrated as lessons rather than oppressive weights in our future!

Christine Caswell
Professor of Journalism and Communication, Boston College
Retired Boston Television Journalist, NBC and ABC

Toby Dorr is a beacon of light for all who've faced tragedy and attempted redemption and reinvention. She reminds us all that while we may have created prisons of our own making, freedom is real and available to us all!

Sara Connell
Author, Founder of Thought Leader Academy

Toby Dorr has an incredible story to share. I was blessed to be her pastor for a transforming time in her life. Her story is one of escape in so many ways. It is filled with twists and turns and irony and spiritual coincidence. It seems that God and the universe have conspired to bring us a story of redemption, second chances, and learning to live with conviction.

Rev. Dr. Chad McMullin

*Living with Conviction* is a true, real-life redemption story. With both humility and courage, Toby Dorr takes full responsibility for the actions that sent her to prison but refuses to let the worst decision of her life determine the rest of her life.

Vulnerable, riveting, and deeply inspiring, this is a story of one who transforms her tragic mistake into a personal mission to help other women avoid going down the same disastrous road that she did. The sensational aspects of this ripped-from-the-headlines story may attract us to read this book, but it's the author's quiet reflections, her dedication to change, and her wholehearted intention to do good for others that make this a transformational story with nuggets of wisdom for any reader.

Betsy Graziani Fasbinder
Author of *Filling Her Shoes*, Podcast Host of The Morning Glory Project: Stories of Determination

Toby does an excellent job taking you behind the walls of the broken prison system and bringing humanity to her fellow inmates. She reveals that beneath the reality of her life altering decisions was the innate desire to be loved, have value, worth and significance. A desire every person can relate to even if your decisions don't result in physical incarceration. Her journey leads to the truth that real freedom comes when we get our love, value and worth in Christ alone.

Gina Hanna
Founder and Director, Beauty for Ashes Ministry

# LIVING WITH
# CONVICTION

---

Unexpected Sisterhood, Healing, and Redemption
In the Wake of Life-Altering Choices

*Nancy,*
*so delightful to meet*
*you! Escape your*
*Prison.*
*Toby Do*

## TOBY DORR

Editor: Lexi Mohney
Senior Editor: Laurie Knight
Cover Design: Jessica Murrell
Publishing Director: Tascha Yoder

An Imprint for GracePoint Publishing (www.GracePointPublishing.com)

GracePoint Matrix, LLC
624 S. Cascade Ave
Suite 201
Colorado Springs, CO 80903
www.GracePointMatrix.com
Email: Admin@GracePointMatrix.com
SAN # 991-6032

A Library of Congress Control Number has been requested and is pending.

ISBN: (Hardcover) 978-1-955272-32-2
ISBN: (Paperback) 978-1-955272-21-6
eISBN: 978-1-955272-22-3

Books may be purchased for educational, business, or sales promotional use.
For bulk order requests and price schedule contact:
Orders@GracePointPublishing.com

## Disclaimer

This book is a memoir. It reflects the author's present recollections of experiences over time. Some names and characteristics have been changed, some events have been compressed, and some dialogue has been recreated. This is a book of memory, and memory has its own story to tell. But it is a truthful story as best memory can provide.

## Content Warning

This book contains writing that some readers may find disturbing, including incidents of physical abuse, strong language, and discussion of suicide.

*To Lucy, Elisa, and Hazel,*
*I wrote this book to inspire women,*
*none more so than you.*

# TABLE OF CONTENTS

# FOREWORD

**THE AFTERNOON I FIRST HEARD** the name Toby Young, she was already long gone. It was February of 2006, and I was working as a young television news anchor and reporter at the CBS affiliate in Kansas City. We'd just gotten word that a wife and mother named Toby might be involved in one of the most bizarre prison breaks in corrections history. Authorities hastily called a news conference and explained that Young, a prison volunteer with no criminal record whatsoever, may have smuggled a prisoner out of Lansing Correctional Facility in a dog crate. I remember thinking two things: *She looks like a librarian, and she must be nuts.*

Over my now-27-year career in broadcast journalism, I have covered it all: murder, tornadoes, bank robberies, explosions, and fires. As a nightside reporter, I had a front row seat to all the whoppers: the woman who faked the birth of sextuplets; the elderly man who robbed a bank to finance an RV for his new girlfriend; the evil pharmacist who watered down life-saving chemotherapy drugs for the love of money. But for years, when people asked me about the craziest story I'd ever covered, I would always reply, "Oh, that's easy, it was the dog crate lady." And I would still answer the same question the same way if it weren't for an article I came across a couple of years ago updating everyone about Toby's journey. She had served her time and was out of prison.

I remember the moment so clearly. At that point in my career, I'd moved on from the horrible hours and rigors of television news and landed my dream job as a daily news talk show host at Kansas City's heritage KMBZ-FM radio station. The new format allowed me to tap into my years of experience covering the news, but with the freedom to talk openly with listeners about countless issues affecting our community. As I read the article detailing Toby's release, I had three rapid-fire thoughts. One, *Holy shit, she's out!* Two, *Toby has grown older, but she looks wiser, more confident.* Three, and most importantly, *I wonder if she'll talk to me.*

Toby did agree to sit down with me, and I am eternally grateful for the lessons she has taught me. I asked her all of the things our community wanted to know. She answered those questions and more. Our meetings grew into a friendship.

If you'd told me back in February of 2006 that I would one day write a foreword to a book by the global headline-grabbing dog crate lady, I would have said you were nuts. I can still see myself standing at the base of the long driveway where Toby once lived—a NO TRESPASSING sign warned reporters and everyone else to keep away from the property—and looking at a home she'd just left behind. I remember thinking, *Who IS this woman? Who flees a house and a husband and two grown kids for a convicted murderer?*

You will find the answer to that question, and so many others, in the pages ahead. Toby shares her life story in unflinching, raw, and brutal honesty. She owns her choices, and she owns the devastation her choices have caused others. But she is also a daily reminder that none of us is as bad as our worst mistake. And she has taught me this: No one is just a headline.

For that, Toby, I thank you. I would like to think we are both older and wiser than we were when our paths first crossed on

February 12, 2006, when I stood at the foot of your driveway, and the FBI had just announced that a manhunt was underway. I wondered where you had gone. Turns out, you and John Manard were already long gone. But your real story was only beginning....

Dana Wright
Journalist and Talk Radio Host on *Dana and Parks*, KMBZ-FM

# Unraveling

unraveling
from the inside out

what was once
tense and silent
is now frayed

and yearning
for voice

pulling apart
breaking down
picking at knots

forging something
new from
the mess

unraveling
will it stop before
I lose the thread
or will I just unravel
and be gone…

Written by Toby while at CCA, December 2007

# DUSTED

SILENT DARKNESS BEGAN TO OFFER a warm hug when sirens and muddled voices pried open a sliver of my consciousness. Streaks of light slashed my vision. I struggled to make sense of moving silhouettes made darker by strobes and blinking colors. Agents closed in. Stinging pain gripped me.

I watched through hissing steam and a heavily fogged, shattered windshield. Thousands of tiny cubes of glass tinkled to my lap, the seat, and the floor as I edged into the moment. I marveled at the limp airbag in my hands and the fine red dust covering me. Angry angles of metal, plastic, and glass cradled me like a mother crocodile harboring her brood in her jaws.

I reached for an unrelenting seat belt pinching at my hips as my nose awoke to the toxic odor of antifreeze. As though through a tunnel, John's reassuring voice eased my transition back to the present.

"Baby, are you alright? I love you, but I have to go before they start shooting."

I shook my head, but my thoughts scattered and drifted like bits of white glitter swirling in a snow globe. Just as my mind seemed to cross the threshold, something primal, something animalistic, some biological necessity induced a higher, more powerful dose of adrenaline. My heart beat faster, but the brutal shock of the crash carved an unexplored union between mind and body—to a place beyond sleep and dreams, to a place more akin to death—where it robbed me of the instinct to breathe.

I willed a shallow wisp of air, and in return, it gave me pain. John got louder, "Baby! Are you okay? I love you Baby. But I gotta go. I've gotta keep you safe. I love you Baby. I love you." Shouldering his door open, he showed his hands, "I'm coming out. Don't shoot."

The tree trunk and the truck hood blurred together through shattered glass and warped plastic. I wiped my eyes; my hands came away with blood. My breath returned slowly along with reality. Vaguely, I remembered the semi. I remembered John throwing his hands in the air as we careened toward the tree.

Brilliant white light from above splashed over the crumpled wreck. Orbs from flashlights bobbed through the woods. Blue and white strobes arced and danced between the ebony trees creating odd ghoulish shadows that appeared and vanished in chaotic choreographies. My body ached; my ears rung.

Dozens of patrol cars howled and flashed. The first officer to my door wore all black, blending with sporadic trees in the night. Taking a tactical position beside the truck, he leaned in through the broken window. I sensed the cold muzzle of a weapon near my ear.

"Get out of the vehicle!" The officer's words were professional and rehearsed, but the stress in his voice conveyed more.

Desensitized, I simply couldn't register the gravity of the moment. I tried to answer but released only a tiny gasp. Then I whispered, "I can't."

"Well, I'll get you outta there!"

Suddenly the seatbelt gave way, and the officer grabbed my hair, pulling me through the opening where a window used to be.

Instinctively, my legs and arms complied with the tremendous force. Like a heavy quilt thrown across a bed, I landed without a wrinkle.

"Facedown! Hands behind your back," an officer yelled.

I turned my head to get precious air. John bellowed, "Baby! Baby! Baby! Are you okay?"

Looking up, I saw him straining against several officers as he dragged them around the end of the truck. John stood in steely defiance; his eyes locked on me. The chopper hovered above, bathing him in glorious light. Leaves and debris blasted away from him as the rotor wash thrashed everything, even his clothes rattled and whipped like a flag in a high wind.

The officer slammed my face against the cold, moist earth. "I said, facedown!"

Once cuffed and pulled to my feet, officers quickly escorted me to a waiting cruiser. Stumbling, I whispered, "I lost my shoe."

"What?" a voice demanded.

"I lost my shoe."

"Well, you won't be needing it."

My confused brain couldn't register what he said, and I repeated, "I lost my shoe."

A different voice in the night commanded, "Let her have her shoe."

They led me to a police car. With my shoes on my feet and new bracelets twisting my arms tightly behind my back, I labored to breathe. I lay across the seat to ease the pressure and closed my eyes. Not until the final siren silenced did it occur to me how deafening the crescendo of chirps had been. The helicopter thrumming overhead faded into the darkness.

For many years, I longed to be noticed, suffocating beneath the weight of invisibility, until John Manard strolled into my life. Then they took him away. I'd never even said goodbye. With handcuffs biting at my wrists, I felt forgotten once again.

Unexpectedly, the door reopened. An officer explained, "We need to move you to another vehicle. This one's outta gas." He firmly tugged me from the car and held my elbow as he pushed me through a myriad of police vehicles and officers.

Suddenly John's face appeared from behind the rear window of a parked vehicle. He rocked the entire car, beating his head against the glass. John held everyone's attention and for a moment, our eyes met. I couldn't quite hear him, but his lips asked, "Are you okay?"

I nodded, and he continued, "Baby, I love you! I love you."

Slapping the top of the car, an officer berated John, "Knock it off."

I strained to keep my eyes on John as more officers stepped between us.

Before I reached the next vehicle, U.S. Marshals intercepted. They uncuffed me and urged me to sign stacks of paper. I obeyed. "Where am I going?"

"To a local jail."

"Wasn't I just in a car wreck?"

"Yes."

"Well, aren't you supposed to go to the hospital when you're in a car wreck?"

"One of the papers you just signed waived your rights to medical care."

"I don't know what any of those papers are. I just signed whatever you gave me."

A heated deliberation between officers ended when the authority that gave me my shoe stated, "Take her to the hospital." Immediately, paramedics appeared, lowered me onto a stretcher, and started buckling a hard plastic collar around my neck.

"What's this for?"

"You might have sustained neck injuries in the wreck; we are stabilizing you until we can get you to the hospital."

I laughed with stifled indignity. "Well," I scoffed, "I've just been pulled through the window of a truck by my hair and then trampled into the dirt by officers. If injuries to my neck are your concern, you're a bit late." The irony, the sheer stupidity, the ridiculousness of my involvement had come full circle as I heard my muffled huffs break into sobs.

The hospital bustled with a frenzied melee. Several hours later, after a doctor okayed my release, officers escorted me through hospital parking. A dark sedan rolled past, stopped, and then slowly backed up.

Mr. U.S. Marshal emerged from the passenger door and walked straight to me. "Toby, you have tough times ahead of you. It's not going to be easy, but don't let this define you. You are so much more than this."

Through speechless tears, I watched my muse walk away.

*How could I live with a conviction?*

# 2.

## A Profound Truth

BLACK AND WHITE PRISON STRIPES brand criminals, and I wore them for my first public appearance. Monday morning, two officers hustled me into the back seat of a patrol car at the tiny Tennessee jail where I'd spent the weekend. A country road wound through forested hills and into a small downtown.

"Can't go that way," the driver said.

Streets were completely blocked. News vans with their satellite dishes extended overflowed the small downtown streets. The female officer suggested, "Let's trick 'em and go 'round the other way before they know what we're doing."

Amused at all the activity, I said, "Isn't it just my luck to be coming to court on a day when something big is going on."

The female officer turned and looked at me incredulously. "Honey, YOU are the star of this show."

My thoughts swirled. For years, I had given many interviews, always well-groomed, well-rehearsed, and polished, but now I was making my biggest public appearance ever, with uncombed hair, black and white stripes of shame, and shackles.

The patrol car pulled around to the back side of the courthouse. A pack of reporters came running around the corner waving microphones and jostling cameras, shouting questions.

The officers handled me from the patrol car toward the courthouse.

From my privileged life, I fell into a bustling pool of hungry sharks. Perhaps my behavior was a bit extreme, maybe even embarrassing, but what was worse than that was that millions watched.

I recognized reporters from Kansas City. At first, I felt relieved to see them, until one thrust a microphone at me, "Were twelve days with John Manard worth ten years of your life?" he yelled above the raucous crowd.

*Ten years?! What does he mean ten years? Ten years in prison????*

I wilted there on the sidewalk; the officers practically dragged me into the building. The media swarmed the door like a hive of angry bees; the officers pushed them out and closed the door firmly behind us.

My stricken expression told the officers I was close to a breakdown, "Let's take a minute. You need to compose yourself. Those rabid reporters would like nothing more than to plaster photos of you with tears streaming and that deer-in-the-headlights look on your face. Now just stop a minute and breathe. Here's what's going to happen. You'll go in the courtroom and the judge will ask you some questions. You answer as you see fit and then we'll take you back to the jail. It won't take more than ten minutes. I'll be right here, and we'll try to avoid the media onslaught on the way out."

I immediately felt relief. *Somebody is on my side. Not everybody hates me. Maybe I can get through this. Yes, I think I can do it.* She guided me, and we did it together. She was right. The judge took only a few minutes to declare that my case must be heard in Kansas.

Grateful to trade my Tennessee cell for one in Kansas, I arrived at the Leavenworth County Jail, just before midnight. Except for the bag of chips in the airport in Memphis, I hadn't eaten since the breakfast I'd barely touched. I waited in an intake room as an officer documented my scant belongings—the items I'd been wearing at the time of my arrest. Prying my locket open, he asked, "What's in here?"

"Oh, be careful with that. It holds a lock of my daughter's hair. She died shortly after birth. I can't replace it if it falls out."

The young officer's demeanor changed instantly. He delicately opened and peeked inside. "It's still there, see? I'm going to put it in a bag, and we'll keep it for you until you leave here."

Another officer brought me a sandwich and watched while I changed into their standard prison uniform, which, thankfully, wasn't Tennessee's black and white. Not much better though—a sickly neon yellow with just a hint of lime green.

She handed me a pair of navy slip-on tennis shoes, which had seen better days, and then escorted me upstairs to a room twice as large as my cell in Tennessee. A bed, a *real* bed, filled half of the wall on the left. A plastic chair sat in the middle of the room and a toilet sat against the half wall of glass that led to the hallway. Oddly, this design gave anyone in the hall a view of an inmate using the toilet. Straight across from the cell, the control hub of the jail allowed officers to check in visitors and man security cameras.

As I settled in and reviewed the day's events in my mind, the door opened. A gray-haired gentleman with a mustache, khaki slacks, and a polo shirt walked in.

"I'm the jail administrator here. Call me Wayne." He reached out to shake my hand. "I want to assure you there will be no reporters gaining access to you inside my jail. We restrict any media. You'll be confined, which means you can't leave here, but unauthorized people will not approach you either. Is there anything I can get you before I go home?"

"Do you have any books? Maybe some Chapstick?"

"I think I can accommodate both of those requests. We'll talk more in the morning. I hope you get some rest."

Minutes later, an officer wheeled a book cart into my room. "Pick anything you'd like. You can have several books at a time." I quickly scanned the two meagerly populated shelves and made my selection.

"Thanks so much! Having a book to read is going to make a big difference."

Another officer walked in and handed me a small plastic jar. "It's lanolin. We don't have Chapstick, but this will work even better. You're in the medical holding room which is right across from our desk and away from the other inmates. In the morning, an officer will take you to the showers. Good night, Ms. Young."

The administrator had come in to meet with me at midnight and utilized his staff to accommodate me. Maybe a few days in this jail—until things were sorted out—wouldn't be so bad. Another step into the unknown, but at least forward.

Heartache, fatigue, and stress pushed me sleeplessly to the wee hours of my first night in Leavenworth. Finally with my eyes closed I relaxed, and memories of John filled my dreams.

*I smuggled a cell phone to John. The lines we had crossed threatened dire consequences for us both, but a cell phone provided us unrestricted contact. By that time, John and I had agreed to attempt the impossible. For those last few weeks before the escape, a future of endless days of wonder together, coupled with elicit cell phone satisfaction, provided incentive to limit our visits.*

*From a quiet, darkened booth in my favorite restaurant not so far from Lansing prison, I cradled a cell phone to my ear and imagined John's presence as his sultry voice delivered desire and need. John, a prisoner confined, lay on a tidy top bunk, his eyes closed. Smooth, clean, confident... hard. John's deprivations, the thought that I could quench his thirst, intoxicated me. John said, "Describe everything, Baby." Something in his request drew me across the line.*

Unashamed, I spoke, "*My tall dewy glass of ice-chilled water twinkles like tiny stars of light.*" I heard John draw a breath and hold it, intent on catching every sound. "*There are people in the nearby shadows who can't quite see us. I hear them talking and dishes clinking. Nobody notices, or cares, that we're together.*" I crunched into a tortilla chip dripping with salsa. John drank in the rhythm of my descriptions of a world beyond his grasp.

My lungs methodically pulled air then squeezed, my heart pulsed as my fingers tingled and my body ached. Duty had sheltered me from the pain of life, yet my obsession with it left no room for passion. John's love poured over me like water on a dying plant. At forty-eight, decades of drought roared to the surface and demanded life. The woman in me craved John's offering.

His words plucked at my heart like liquid lyrics. John's voice resonated deep within me from across town. The fantasy took me on a meteoric ride.

We laughed. We loved.

"*Outside the window, people are hunting for spaces closer to the door. They hop out and zip their coats higher and pull hats lower to avoid the blustering cold weather.*"

I paused when the waitress stood at my table to refill my soda and wait for my order. John heard her presentation and said, "*Get some queso, Baby. I love queso!*"

"*Wow, John, this plate is hot. I almost burned my finger.*"

John didn't miss the opportunity to tease me, "*She said it was hot, Baby, just like you.*"

"*I know, I know. But I just had to move it a bit.*"

"*I wish I was there next to you.*"

"*There's steam rising off the plate and vanishing into the darkness. Steak. Medium rare.*"

"*Oh, that's how I like it too, Baby! Oh, cut into its center and let the juices run out. Nice and red. I can taste it, Baby. It's so good!*"

"*John, it's so tender.*" I lift my fork; I hear him breathe, and I close *my eyes.*

*Driven by sheer desire, as if by some astral projection, I feel John sitting with me. I imagine his smile and his hair—thick, flaming red hair.*

*I lift my glass. "To us."*

*"To us, Baby. To us." John's contraband cellphone opened a whole new world in our relationship. Vicariously, he lived for our excursions.*

*"Where are we going today, Baby?" John started every day with this simple question. I bought wireless earphones so my hands could be free while I took John with me.*

*"Let's go to Nebraska Furniture Mart. You won't believe how big this place is!"*

*"Describe everything you see."*

*"There's the cutest little girl with wild curls and a purple corduroy jumper. She's chattering non-stop, and her mom has so much patience, stopping to let her look at anything that catches her fancy."*

*"I see her, Baby. I can see her. She's adorable."*

*"Oh, John, look. Here's a rocking chair for two. It's black leather and the leather is smooth and soft like butter. When I sit in it, it glides more than it rocks. I could sit here and read forever. I could read to you! All my favorite books."*

*"Baby, I love it too. We'll buy that chair for you and me to sit in together. Let's go look at lamps to put over our black leather chair-for-two. And beds—we won't need a king-size bed, we'll cuddle into a full-size one."*

*On the nights Rob was at the fire station, my phone calls with John took on an entirely different tone. John made me crazy for his touch, and I could hardly stand not being with him. He'd sing to me softly while I fell in and out of sleep. We were together as much as any couple could be. We talked about everything. I fell in love with his strong voice, his endless patience to listen to all the stories of my life, and his ability to empathize with every word. Rob had never done that.*

*"Oh, Baby, the sun's coming up. Gotta go for count."*

*The lack of sleep, along with the frenzy of desire made me delirious. I couldn't wait for February 12, the day we'd really be together. I was excited and nervous and filled with anticipation to play out all that we'd discussed. At that point, nothing could make me refuse.*

Trays clanged out in the hallway. Images of the last few days, the escape, the truck, John's hands on the wheel, the stress in his voice, the high-speed car chase, the tree, the flashing lights, the handcuffs, the separation, and that Tennessee courthouse debacle, slammed into my consciousness. I woke with a start and looked around me. *Where am I?*

*It's all real. Not a dream. We did it. We pulled it off. We were together. I woke in his arms. The candlelit bubble baths. The fireplace. The music. And look where I am now...*

Alone. Lost and alone. Both of us locked up, behind different bars on different sides of town.

*Who would bring the world to me as I had for John?*

# 3.

## THE SHADOW CAST

**MEALS ARRIVED ON A TRAY**, delivered by a group of male inmates wearing green and white striped clothing. I soon learned that these were the jail's trustees tasked with menial jobs like mopping floors, delivering meals, and emptying trash. In return, they were allowed access to an outdoor rec area and extended privileges in their own pod.

Breakfast consisted of rubbery fake eggs and a piece of bread. Lunch brought sandwiches with either mustard or mayonnaise. When a particular trustee discovered that I preferred mustard, he made sure I got mustard every day. Unfortunately for the rest of the jail, it meant they all got mustard as well.

I flashed back to the mustard happy faces I drew on my sons' sandwiches. I missed my boys desperately.

*What must they be thinking?*

The visiting area and medical exam rooms were to my left and the rest of the jail to the right. Every inmate needing medical attention or going to a visit passed by my cell. Inmates in different colored outfits paraded past all day long.

When Wayne stopped in, I said, "I noticed your book cart isn't very full. Do you take book donations?"

"Sure. As long as they're paperbacks. I don't need anyone

slamming someone with a hardback book. Anyway, you should have a court date coming next week, and I think you're set to have a visit today. Your parents are anxious to see you."

Mom and Dad were on their way. What words could I share? I couldn't explain what I didn't understand. Barely a week had passed since agents ended my time on the run. I couldn't imagine any punishment strong enough to diminish the shame I'd feel in Dad's presence. I dreaded and craved their visit.

Wearing jail scrubs, and my hair frazzled, I followed an officer, head down and tears brimming.

"Ms. Young, you're in room three."

As I pulled the door open, Mom and Dad and one of my sisters were on the other side of the glass, but I simply couldn't lift my eyes to look at them. My sister took the phone, I felt her impatience through the glass coercing me to put the receiver to my ear as I took a seat on the small metal stool. The black hole within me swallowed the joyful smile I would have offered in any other circumstances.

"Are you okay?" she asked.

I nodded almost imperceptibly.

She continued, "I'm mad that you left me." She handed the phone to Dad and walked out of the room as if walking out of my life.

*Mad? Mad at me? But I'm back. Why would you be mad? Here I am. Don't you see me? Don't you love me?*

Dad's eyes still loved me, "Toby we're going to get through this. We'll be right here with you, but I want you to know you can do this. Whatever it is. You can do this, and your mother and I will be right here with you every step of the way."

"Daddy..."

Mom took the phone last. She put her hand on the glass and I spread mine on the other side, matching her finger to finger. "Toby, I'm not mad at you. I'm just glad you're back. I love you."

"Mom." I wiped my tears to see her more clearly. Embarrassed, I struggled for words.

*They had to know John and I had sex. It's all the news talked about. Oh, my gosh! Even my most private things were no longer private. Those black satin sheets plastered on the news...*

"Mom..."

"We're here Toby. We'll take care of everything. But we can't stay any longer. They only gave us thirty minutes, but we're going to get that changed. You just rest and try not to worry. We'll figure this all out. You're not alone. I love you, Toby. I'm glad you're back. Safe. And that's all that matters. Anything else we can deal with."

Behind the scenes, my family scrambled to find an attorney and learn as much as they could about the court process. My youngest brother's best friend since first grade was an attorney; they approached him for guidance. During the conversation, Jim offered to take my case. He didn't have a lot of experience with criminal cases, but everyone felt comfortable with his council.

I remembered Jim as a child pushing around his sister's baby stroller. Filled with baseball bats and gloves, he declared he was going to start a ball team. Jim sounded like a good choice to me if only for the history we shared.

"Young, you have court at ten o'clock." Leavenworth County wasted no time getting me in front of a judge.

*Court! What a nightmare that Tennessee court appearance turned out to be. What will it be like here? Hopefully nobody knows about it, and it will be a short, quiet hearing after which I'll be allowed to go home.*

With only one outfit and no makeup to apply, I didn't need to prepare. Officers arrived to escort me. The courthouse shared the same roof as the jail.

*Brilliant design. They should all be this way. No transports and no lines of media to navigate...*

A secret warren of concrete corridors allowed inmates to appear discreetly in a courtroom through a hidden side door like rabbits from their dens. I loved this level of security and felt comfortable being hidden away where I couldn't be ambushed by the media. I hadn't talked to Jim yet but knew he'd be waiting in the courtroom for me.

*It's nice to know somebody will be on my side in there. Somebody I know and trust. I can do this. Let's get it over with.*

Unprepared for a courtroom full of media, I blinked at the standing-room-only crowd. I wanted to look for my parents but didn't want to face the reporters, so I kept my eyes on the judge. Things were uneventful—a lot of protocol and legalese, until Jim said, "Your Honor, I've only just taken this case and haven't had time to prepare. I'd like to ask for a two-week continuance to talk to my client and prepare her case."

*Two weeks? Wait a minute. Aren't I going home today?*

I folded in on myself as I heard the judge's gavel, and my officers ushered me through the side door back into the warren.

Sitting on my bed with a head full of questions and eyes full of tears, my world crashed in on me.

*Two weeks! Nobody even mentioned two weeks. This is a mistake. Somebody needs to fix it. I'm supposed to be going home. Right now. Home. Nobody mentioned two weeks!*

"Young, you have an attorney visit."

*Thank goodness. Jim is coming to tell me how he's going to fix this.*

Next to the visiting area, the small, square attorney conference room with glass walls contained a standard metal desk with chairs on either side where I fell into Jim's arms sobbing.

"Our conversations in here are not recorded. First, I must ask you, are you okay with me representing you?"

"Yes. Of course. But, Jim, two weeks—what does that mean?

I can't stay in here for two weeks!"

"Toby, I don't think you know how crazy it is out there. The media is camped at the end of your driveway and your parents' driveway. They hound your sisters daily for comments. Your family posted 'No Trespassing' signs to keep the reporters at bay. You should be glad to be in here."

"Surely, it can't be that bad."

"Toby, the media is relentless. I think you'd find the intrusion worse than being in jail. Being locked up is safe, and this time will count towards any sentence you may get."

My brief experiences with the media had been overwhelming. I pictured them waiting like vultures at the end of my parents' quarter-mile-long driveway, hoping to ambush someone.

*But wait. What did Jim just say? My time would count towards a sentence. A prison sentence?*

"Time? You think I'll have to do time?"

Jim nodded, "I don't know for sure, and I'll do everything I can to keep you out. I haven't talked to the prosecutor yet to know what he's thinking. But it is possible. Can you just sit tight for two weeks while I figure some things out?"

I knew Jim. My whole family knew Jim. We trusted him. "Okay, I'll stay here for two weeks."

"Toby, you might be here for longer than two weeks, but we can start there. Bail is a possibility, but I would recommend against it. It really is crazy out there. I'm not sure you could handle it."

Back in my room my mind ran wildly away from logic, yet strangely towards acceptance.

*Any sentence I get?*

*"They don't put people like you in prison," John said.*

*Deep down I knew it. I knew it all along. Of course, they're going to put me in jail—well they did, actually. Here I am. But maybe they'll want prison time as well... Could I do time? Sitting here alone in a medical holding room was one thing, but time—real time—in prison with a bunch of angry, crazy women? Could I do that kind of time?*

"Young, you have another legal visit."

*Jim's back? Maybe he's already figured something out!*

A stranger waited in the attorney visiting room. "Ms. Young, I'm a bail bondsman and I need to gather some information to provide a recommendation to the judge."

Sweat beaded on his dark skin and his shirt stretched around his belly to the point of popping at the buttons. His excitement seemed out of place.

"Do you have a passport?"

"No."

"A driver's license?"

"Yes."

"Own a home?"

"With my husband."

"I've never had a case this big!"

*Ahhh, now I see the reason for his excitement. Surely, I can't be the biggest case in the history of Leavenworth County. How long has he been doing this job?*

"I'm thinking a million dollars. Yep. A million-dollar bond. That's what I'm going to recommend."

I stared at him, "A million dollars?"

Slapped in the face with some cold hard facts, I realized Jim was right.

I'd just stay in jail. I didn't have a million dollars, anyway, if that's what it took to get me out.

"Okay then, are we done?" I refused to sit there like a notorious VIP and be gawked at by this paparazzi-styled bondsman who was simply intrigued by the shadow I cast.

Standing, I walked out of the room, into the secure area of the jail where he couldn't follow, leaving him flapping at me, "Ms. Young... Ms. Young."

I kept walking.

Back in my room, I paced.

*Looks like I won't be going home after all. A million dollars! Might as well be no bail at all. A fucking million dollars. How can I deal with staying here? I'll read practically every book on their meager little cart by the end of the month. What will I do then? Start over, I guess. Read them all twice. I have to do more than just read though, I need something to do. That's it!*

I started writing letters to people I'd worked with, to friends of my parents, and organizations I'd been a part of. "Do you have any paperback books you wouldn't mind passing on? The jail here accepts donations, and they only have a handful of books in their library. It would make a world of difference to inmates if they had books to read to pass their time."

Now that was a project worth my time.

**4.**

## My Quandary

**THREE WEEKS INTO MY JAIL STAY**, Wayne walked into my room. "Ms. Young, there's a couple of things we need to discuss."

"Okay," I leaned in, "What's going on?"

"First of all. Thank you for your book drive. We now have an entire room filled with books. Please stop. We can't handle any more."

"That's great! Okay, no more letters requesting books. What's next?"

Wayne looked over his glasses at me, "Why are you still here? I expected you to be gone long before now."

"I expected that, too, but here I am."

"Why, though? Why haven't you bonded out?"

I waved my hand, "Oh, take your pick. The hordes of media camped out at my parents' driveway. Or maybe the million-dollar bond…"

"I doubt your bond is a million dollars."

"Well, that's what he said, and I don't have it. Not even close. Looks like I'm staying put for however long this takes."

"Well, you're in my medical observation room, and I need to have it back for medical cases."

"Okay, so what do we do now?"

20

Wayne sighed, "I'm going to move you to seg."

"Seg! No, you're not. I haven't broken any rules. You don't have a reason to put me in seg. I'm not going." Segregation was punishment within punishment, jail within jail. Hell within hell. Locked down twenty-three hours a day. Alone. People went crazy in seg.

"For your own protection. Those women are street smart. You won't stand a chance in general population. They'll beat you up because you have a candy bar and they don't. I can't protect you in there."

"I'm not requesting protective custody. I'm not going to seg. I'll take my chances. I think I'll be alright. How about if I let you know if I'm having trouble."

Shaking his head, Wayne left my room and came back with a paper for me to sign. "This states that you have refused segregation, even after we advised it for your own safety. We can't be held responsible for anything that happens to you in general population."

"Deal!" I said, signing with a flourish. "When am I going?"

"This afternoon. And by the way, you need to stop hugging your attorney."

I packed the few things I had and waited. I felt strong as I advocated for what I wanted. I could have given in and spent my time as a mouse in hiding, but I resolved to face general population—and life behind bars.

Even with my newfound bravado, my legs shook as I walked down the hall to the women's pod. Some of the women passed on their way to visits, and they often waved at me.

Stopping outside a small metal door, the officer called into his radio and the door swung open to a large, bright, sun-filled room. There were no windows, but two large skylights bathed the space with light. Several payphones hung on the wall to the left of the door. Metal tables and benches bolted to the floor filled the open space. Wide metal stairs led to a catwalk along the back wall where doors opened to cells. Showers were in the back right corner. A TV mounted high on the wall, well out of reach, occupied the women's time.

Entering the pod, conversations ceased as the women turned to look at me. Then, as if directed to begin in unison, an avalanche of questions swept over me.

"Wondered when they'd finally send you down here," a tiny woman said. "We seen you on the news! We all know why you're here. I'm in here for dope. Not my first time neither."

"Yeah, you're on the TV all the time—like every night..."

"Hey! You're the Dog Lady," an elderly Black woman called. Her short silvery hair was brushed back in a close cut, and she seemed to watch over the other women in a grandmotherly fashion. Her voice held quiet authority; a power relinquished by the others.

The officer asked, "Who has an open bunk?"

A dark-haired girl, far too young to be in jail, answered, "I do. She can be in with me. Come on, I'll show you."

The officer turned to leave while I exhaled the breath of panic that threatened to block my next breath.

*This doesn't seem so bad...*

Each cell had a narrow opaque window which revealed day or night. Nothing else could be seen. In jail, lights are never turned off completely. I read books in the middle of the night with no strain at all. This odd, twenty-four-hour light cycle made routine difficult, and with sleeping allowed throughout the day, it created a disturbance in the routine I so cherished when I was free.

Our cell, on the second tier and farthest from the entrance, contained four beds—two lower bunks and two uppers. No ladders. I wondered about the physical strength needed to raise and lower myself. My new roommate, Jessica, pointed to her lower bunk. "That's my bed. The rest are open. Take your pick."

I chose the other lower bunk and sat down. The noise from the dayroom suddenly shifted from undertones of television noise and the brushy sounds of conversation to a shuffle of women making their way to their rooms; doors clanged shut from both ends of the corridor.

I looked at my new roommate with a question on my face.

"Count time," she said. "We have to wait in our cells while they count us, and when they're done, we can go back out into the pod."

*Ah, yes, count time. I hadn't been on this side of it before. Count time controlled my clandestine conversations with John.*

After being in my new cell for just a few minutes, I realized Jessica talked non-stop and had no filters.

"I know what you're in here for. I never met anyone famous before. I'm in here because I robbed a delivery driver. I called for some Chinese food and when the driver came, I robbed him with a knife. I only got seven bucks. And the food. I sat on the porch and waited for the police to show up. I don't know why I robbed that delivery driver except that I just needed to do it. I have a little dog. I love my dog. I think my dog doesn't know why I'm gone. I just want to go home and be with my dog. My dog loves me, he's just a little dog. He might be the only person in the whole world who loves me. Well, I know my mom loves me. And my dad. I love my dad a lot."

I commented, "Dads are special, I know mine is. He's dying."

Jessica leaned in, so I continued, "Last summer, Dad went to the hospital for some tests, and they found stage four bladder cancer. Stage four. That means it's too late. No real treatment, just make the best of what time you have left. My sisters are determined to beat that cancer though and started calling the Mayo Clinic and every other cancer center they could find. I tried to intercede. Why put Dad through all the sickness of chemo when maybe he should just live life for however long he has left?

Dad set up his retirement so that there are no survivor benefits. When he dies, his pension stops. My mom's pension is something like a hundred dollars a month plus social security, but nowhere near what their living expenses are. Dad decided that enjoying whatever time he had left didn't matter. Getting more pension payments did. So, he chose chemo."

"I think I love your dad." Jessica commented.

"Everyone does. He's a superhero. When I was five years old, he got burned in our backyard in an accident. He was in the hospital for six months. He nearly died. But that burn gave him extraordinary strength. My dad doesn't back down from anything."

*Like the sun, he centered my family. My world rose and set on what Dad thought; his opinions confirmed worthy ideas. The prospect of life without him was unbearable.*

Uncomfortable with the silence, Jessica continued her litany, "I cut myself. See my arms? I don't know why I cut myself except it lets the pain out. I don't know why I do lots of things. I hear voices, they tell me to do crazy things, mostly to hurt people. I would never hurt my dog. I love my little dog. I hope he doesn't hate me because I'm in here. Do you think he'll remember me? I don't know why I hear voices. Do you hear voices? I do and I have to do what the voices say because they just get louder and louder and louder until I can't stand the sound anymore. I do what they say so they'll leave me alone. I'm supposed to be on meds, lots of meds, but they took all of them away when they put me in here and now the voices are coming back. They tell me to hurt people, but I don't think I'll hurt you. I think I like you. Wanna play cards?"

"Of course I want to play cards!" Anything to keep those voices—and Jessica—quiet.

*This poor little girl. Maybe she is crazy, but she seems more lost than crazy. And desperate to talk to someone. Well, listening is one thing I can do for her. Those voices are a bit frightening. I'm not sure if*

*I should be afraid or not. I've never known anyone who heard voices. Does the staff here know about those voices? Why did they take away her medications if they kept the voices under control? Is Jessica a ticking time bomb? And I'm locked in here with her. How long would it take for someone to come here and help me if I needed it? Our room is the farthest from the pod door. I can't change that, and I can't change where I am, but I can be Jessica's friend. I think that's what she needs more than anything. Just in case, I'll stay awake until she falls asleep. She outweighs me by at least 150 pounds. I'm not sure I'd have the upper hand in a physical confrontation.*

We played cards until three o'clock in the morning our first night. I learned that Jessica had been in and out of mental hospitals for most of her nineteen years. She wanted to be a good girl, but she was driven by demons which made it difficult. Thankfully, I could not relate.

I did have my own demons—duty, perfectionism, an all-consuming need to be loved and appreciated—but at least mine didn't speak.

Time passed. Jail tedium became my new norm. Women, barely in their twenties, categorized by charges of prostitution, crack cocaine, and sometimes meth, provided community.

Angie, a tiny little thing with thick, dark hair and Vicky, a mousy blond with a raggedly self-cut pixie, kept the pod entertained with their constant bickering.

Vicky worried about her "ghetto golds"—dental decorations confiscated during her arrest. "Do you think they'll be there when I get out? I paid a lot of money for those."

Angie quickly replied, "Who cares? They look stupid anyway."

They were friends of a sort, frequenting the same crack houses on the streets and turning tricks. Occasionally, they placed collect calls to regular customers, begging for money on their books in return for future favors. Surprisingly, most of the time it worked. Then they'd get into arguments about who brought the most money into their jail accounts.

Angie loved to taunt Vicky, "At least on the streets, I get paid cash for mine. I don't turn tricks for dope. I wouldn't stoop that low."

"I get paid sometimes." Vicky retorted.

"Not many." Angie answered back.

Vicky never tried to remove herself from Angie's circle. In fact, she chased her around like a lost puppy begging for attention. The rest of the women in the pod separated them before any violence broke out. Truthfully though, I don't think Vicky had a fight in her. Angie could probably hold her own with anyone, but Vicky was a total pushover.

Every few weeks the same debate would rekindle. "At least I don't turn tricks for dope…"

Ruby, the elderly Black woman would intercede. "That's all we need, is the po-leece comin' in here and lockin' us all down over your stupid shit. A trick is a trick. Ain't nuthin' makes one more worser than another."

Inmates played the blame game. They pointed fingers. They found excuses for their troubles. They worked hard to avoid responsibility, but they never grew. They yearned for self-respect and direction, so, instinctively, they gathered around me. My stories of training dogs, riding horses, working a high-level corporate job and being a mother were different from the stories they knew.

Despite the monotony, the routine soothed me. No analysis. No decisions. No responsibility. Morning pill call. Breakfast. Shower time. Clean the pod. Lunch. Nap. Dinner. TV. Evening pill call. Cards. Bed.

Morning pill call.

Breakfast.

Shower time.

Clean the pod.
Lunch.
Nap.
Dinner.
TV.
Evening Pill Call.
Cards.
Bed.

Sometimes, though, things blew up. And when they did—because of the monotony of our lives—they were monumental...

5.

## BREAKDOWN

**THE SYSTEM NULLIFIED US IN** multiple ways. In jail, all outside items were prohibited, including prescriptions. Jail doctors re-evaluated and re-prescribed whatever they thought necessary, often disregarding medical history completely.

As inmates, we had no patients' rights, and most didn't care, we were unseen. With limited budgets and an eye on the ever-inadequate bottom line, the needs of the inmates weren't important.

Thankfully, my parents obtained a judge's order to allow my thyroid medication.

Many, like Jessica, required medications to manage their mental illnesses. Most inmates didn't have families to advocate for their rights in a courtroom. It is not recommended to abruptly stop psych medications cold turkey, but in the absence of a staff psychiatrist, jails leave many inmates to spiral deeper into their illness. Standard policy treated psych meds as any other prescription, denied upon admission.

Every morning, pill call administered my thyroid pill. For Jessica, pill call reminded her that she was on her own for another day of tormented psychosis.

"Anything for me?" she would call out hopefully from the

open door of our cell.

"Nothing for you," came the reply.

One morning as I climbed the stairs after pill call, I heard Jessica's frustration boiling over into an uncontrollable rage. I ran to our room. Jessica slapped the intercom button over and over, "I need my fuckin' pills! These voices are getting louder and louder. I can't stop them anymore. I'm going to do something I can't stop myself from doing. I don't want to do it! I need my fuckin' pills!"

"Jessica, calm down. Stop. You're gonna get in trouble. Just calm down."

She pounded her fists against the concrete, then she rammed her forehead into the wall. "Why won't they listen to me? Why can't I have my pills? Toby, I need help!"

I felt no fear for my own safety, yet in that moment, Jessica changed. Her savage appearance manifested a primal spirit, the likes of which I'd never seen. The feral voices in Jessica's head transformed her into a sub-human version of herself, but then, with my compassionate hand on her back, she dissolved into a weeping defeated child.

"I need help. I need help."

"I know you do, Jessica, but this isn't the way." Her long dark hair clung to her sweaty face.

In her moment of resolve, the door burst open, and officers stormed the room. They grabbed her arms and spun her around. Her forehead resembled the mushy pulp of a half-cut grapefruit. Her fists were like those of a bare-knuckled brawler. "Hands behind your back!"

I could stand no more and launched a defense. "Stop! She doesn't need to be arrested. Jessica needs help. Look at her hands, they're all swollen and bloody. Go get ice. I'll calm her down."

More shocking than my outburst, the officers obeyed. They

released her and left. In a few moments, one of them returned with gel ice packs.

Jessica collapsed into me as I supported her head, and she sobbed. "Why won't they get me my meds, Toby? I need help. I'm not strong enough to stop these voices."

Eventually, she settled as I slid the hair away from her face and held the ice packs on her bloodied hands.

Our pod remained on lockdown. A long hour passed as I soothed my cell mate and then myself. We sat in silence for a moment, as I searched for a story to distract her. "I found significance in my work at the prison, running the dog program. My sons were off to college and the silence of my empty nest at home overwhelmed me—it had been smothered by an emotionless, loveless marriage of convenience, abandoned to circumstances beyond repair. Neither of us could navigate back to one another.

"One night we got a call from the hospital telling us Dad had been rushed into emergency surgery. We waited all night until they brought Dad back to the ICU. We could see him for only a few minutes. I left and went straight to the prison where John Manard waited. He took one look at me and asked what was wrong. I told him about Dad, and he said that it was a good thing I had my husband with me because it would have been hard to drive with all that on my mind. I told John that my husband didn't come. He'd said he couldn't do anything at the hospital and there was no sense in both of us losing sleep. It sounded logical when my husband said it, but when I repeated it back to John, the stunned look on his face forced me to see it for the cruel and selfish thing it was."

Jessica asked, "What did John say?"

"He asked me why I was still married to him."

"And your answer?"

"I didn't have one. That bothered me the most. When

30

pressed, I couldn't think of a single reason why I was still married. Shouldn't I have an instant answer to that question? Wouldn't someone in a loving marriage not have to think about it? That question opened Pandora's box. I'd spent years advocating and promoting the myth of my perfect life. Now, my blinders had been ripped off: I couldn't unhear that question: 'Why are you still married to him?' Even more troubling I couldn't even invent an answer. He caught me off guard."

I paused for a long moment while we both stared. My voice remained silent as my mind raced. *Neither common sense nor courtesy saved us from our wedding duty, so we bought a house, started a family, and settled in. The first months of my marriage proved different than the close-knit, rough and tumble, talking over each other, throwing footballs, and playing volleyball, croquet or tag, antics in the backyard to which I'd grown accustomed. Ill-equipped to handle isolation, I yearned for my husband's presence.*

*Rob played golf every Saturday with his friends while I worked household chores and projects alone. I wondered,* How long does one game of golf take, for heaven's sake? *After a month, I took action.*

*Eagerly, I could barely wait to share with Rob. "Guess what?"*

*Rob rested his clubs in the closet with a disinterested expression, so I sprung the surprise, "I signed up for golf lessons today! Isn't that awesome?"*

*Rob's face reflected his thoughts but that wasn't enough for him, so he looked at me and said, "Well, that's nice, Toby, but before you go to all that trouble, you'd better find someone to golf with, golfing alone is no fun."*

*"I thought I'd golf with you." My mouth uttered the words, but my ears heard a hurt, pouty little girl.*

*"No. I golf with my friends."*

*His words cut the breath from my lungs. I recoiled from the pain, as a five-year-old little girl thrust up to the surface to shelter me and take charge. She knew to crack a whip and send me to complete my duties. Work would make me feel needed, work would show Rob and the world that I am necessary.*

And so there I sat, alone, until Jessica shook me from the past, "Toby, are you okay?"

"My husband didn't notice how much Dad's cancer affected me, but John Manard did. He saw right into my soul. I'd been waiting all my life for someone to see me, to notice me, to love me; John did. He waited eagerly for me to show up at the prison. I conducted business as usual, but now, the time between working with dogs flourished with searing conversations about life and purpose and love. My inability to answer John's question blinked a green light, an open door to love."

"I want to be loved!" Jessica proclaimed, her mind totally distracted from her voices and her lack of medications.

I paused, reflecting on a new truth. "I don't know what I'm going to do. Can I stay in this marriage? I don't think it can be saved. I'm not even sure I want to try. Crazier still, during the escape, I thought, 'at least they'll let me get a divorce now.' That's an eye-opener."

The harsh sound of the intercom interrupted our moment, "Young, pack your things. We're moving you."

Jessica's tears returned, "Now look what I've done. I'm losing the only friend I've ever had. I don't want you to leave," she wailed. Jessica, the fragile child whom I cared about, dissolved.

"I'll be just down the hall, Jessica. We can still play cards and hang out in the dayroom. I won't be far."

I gathered my few belongings and left the cell.

The solid metal doors operated remotely from a central control unit which, when unlocked, released its constant tension, and the door sprung away from the frame. This cell door behavior was an industry standard. Inmates called it "popping the door."

Close to midnight the next day, a guard popped my door and woke me from a deep sleep. Jessica stood there with an officer.

"We're moving her out to get help, but she wants to say goodbye."

Jessica hugged me fiercely, "I brought you my things. Maybe you can use them. You're my only friend."

She handed me a ragged long underwear shirt—hardly worth saving—her used deodorant, an unopened candy bar, and a couple of stamps. They represented her only possessions in the whole world—except for her little dog. She left them to me. In her mind, she gave me everything.

"Jessica, I'm not going to use your things, but I will keep them safe for you."

"They're taking me to the mental hospital. Now maybe I can get these voices stopped. I'll never forget you, Toby." She repeated, "You're my only friend."

"You'll see me again, Jessica. I'll be here waiting for you when you come back. Take care of yourself and do what the doctors say. I love you, Jessica."

I stepped out of my cell and onto the catwalk to watch my roommate walk out of the pod. She turned and waved over her shoulder and mouthed the word, "Bye." She reminded me of a little child in an adult's body leaving for her first day of school.

Having finally opened up to someone about Dad's illness and the emptiness of my marriage, I felt a weight lift. I realized with John pulling on my heart, mind, and soul to relax and fall for the first time in my life, I complied and let myself plunge into the forbidden. The five-year-old girl inside me screamed in protest at the inevitability of watching her daddy die. I escaped. I ran away, believing I could stop another loss.

Many people believe the heart is a fickle thing, but I know that's not true. Dad's mortality pushed me away from my painful past, while John tempted me towards a future filled with affection. I could see and feel the freshness and wonder of things that were childlike in my new world with John. The influence of our time together was enormous. Clarity blossomed. Like the dogs needing rescue, attention, treats, and the affection of someone to cuddle and pet and love, I realized that the life I led was void of all those things too.

Finally, someone wanted to rescue me. At the most barren intersection in my life, he had the time to invest and wait and immerse himself in me. He spied my need and took the opportunity to reach deep inside to taste the untouched secrets that I'd been hiding for decades. My heart wasn't fickle—it was dying. And John shocked it back to life with a rationalism that could only be described as romantic.

Our conversations awakened me to the sense that more existed in my dying self than I'd known. I fell into one vulnerable conversation after another. Sharing pain and heartaches, we found comfort and strength in every dark hallway with loving pups as our alibi. Love hijacked my reason, and I chased John blindly until I arrived behind bars, facing a conviction.

Love found me fully and completely. I couldn't deny myself or argue with my heart, regardless of common sense. I found the one person who would risk anything and everything for me. No matter what the future brought, at least I knew the love and passion of romance, worthiness, value, and acceptance.

Even if only for twelve days.

# 6.

## PEANUT BUTTER KITES

**EACH MORNING AT BREAKFAST**, I jerked back to my present reality. Prison meals were prepared across town, stacked into groups of twenty plastic trays, and loaded into a delivery truck to be shipped and delivered to each pod. The plastic sealed containers cooled and condensed the food into soggy, tasteless, colorless mush that wafted with offensive odors to ruin my appetite before I even sat down.

The fake rubber eggs offered no relief to my increasing hunger. Sandwiches revealed greenish, slimy meat that looked like a *Fear Factor* challenge. Dinnertime served rice or pasta with a protein called *guess-the-meat*. Most days, it became a game of identification.

On one occasion, Tina found a complete chicken foot in her dinner. Screaming in disgust, we passed the foot around, flexing its ligaments causing the toes to walk in midair. Needless to say, no one ate it, but an officer swooped in like an eagle to grab the evidence from our play to discard and deny its existence.

Because of a severe case of IBS, Angie's digestive system protested in pain every time she ate processed meat filled with sodium nitrites and curing solutions. She got the luxury of peanut butter every day for lunch. My mouth watered at the sight of its luxurious smooth texture, rich color, and delicious exotic smell, so I tried to broker a meal deal: my dessert for her cup of peanut butter. Most days the dessert didn't make the cut, and she quickly declined the trade. I coveted her peanut butter like I was starving in a desert.

Peanut butter. Peanut butter. Peanut butter. Obsessed and delirious, I searched for solutions.

I approached one of the officers at lunch. "How can I get peanut butter?"

"The peanut butter is for vegetarians."

"Do they get peanut butter every day?"

"Yes, for lunch."

The next day, when lunch was served, I told the officer, "I'm a vegetarian."

"You weren't a vegetarian yesterday."

"Well, I am today."

Wayne walked into our pod later that afternoon. He sighed. "Ms. Young, you aren't a vegetarian."

"Yes, I am."

"Do you have a medical note from a doctor saying you're a vegetarian?"

"Being a vegetarian isn't a medical condition. It's a choice. I choose to be vegetarian."

"You weren't a vegetarian yesterday. Why the change?"

"Peanut butter."

He sighed again, "Okay, sign this form saying you're a vegetarian, and we'll start you on a vegetarian diet tomorrow. But you won't get any meat for breakfast or for dinner."

"Will I get peanut butter?"

"Yes," he replied wearily, shaking his head. "Every day for lunch."

"I can live with that."

Until I realized I couldn't; a small cup of peanut butter

couldn't slake my peanut butter thirst or fill my belly. I hated the bland beans that were slopped on my plate for dinner. I studied the commissary sheet more closely… candy bars, ramen noodles…

I refused to be a peanut butter victim.

*If we could buy peanut butter on commissary, none of us would be hungry again. But how? How could a muzzled, insignificant inmate change the world?*

As it turned out, the jail system already had a tool in place. Kites: the inmate slang for some boringly named administrative form designed as a tool for inmates to submit requests to the administrator.

My mind immediately flew back to the days in grassy fields with Dad. I remembered his swift steps dashing back and forth between my siblings and me while he kept our kites airborne. Seen for miles, kites could not be ignored. I knew then I had to file a kite.

*Go file a kite if you want a new blanket that wasn't threadbare and full of holes. Go file a kite if your light is flickering. Go file a kite if your toilet is plugged or your toothache escalates to a number twelve on the scale of pain, or the caged ceiling light buzzed and flickered to epileptic distraction all night long.*

*Go file a kite because the administrator cannot ignore the request.*

My kite could not be ignored, but it could be dismissed without sufficient merit. How could I make it significant enough to evoke action? How could I make this kite fly?

"Hey girls, don't you think we should have some more options on this commissary form?" I asked.

"Yes! I want Twizzlers."

"Can we get Pop Tarts?"

"I have an idea, grab a stack of kites, and have a seat. I'm going to write a kite demanding some healthy food choices and more hygiene products on the commissary. When I'm done, each of you copy what I've written, on your own kite. We'll all file our kites together."

"I can't write that well. Can you write it for me, Miss Toby?" Butterfly asked.

Butterfly, a revolving jail regular without a real name, couldn't make sense of a written word longer than four letters, and she couldn't read cursive at all. I'd been helping her learn to write and read better. With first-grade writing skills, she leaned on me to do it for her, but kites didn't work that way. The administrator would recognize my handwriting and dismiss her request, lessening the impact of our united front. "No, it must be in your writing, Butterfly. Just take your time and do the best you can. It doesn't have to be perfect."

We stuffed that box with more than two dozen kites. Giddy with excitement over our decision to force a change, we waited.

And waited…

"Okay girls, gather round. We're going to write another kite, and we're going to write one every day until we're heard."

Our kite box bulged, and officers shook their heads every night as they emptied it.

One morning a trustee came in to change a lightbulb, and Angie said, "Miss Toby, why are there only men trustees? I want to be a trustee. I'd like to have a job to do—and we could go outside."

"Get the kites," I commanded.

Each inmate wrote by hand:

> *The current trustee program is a form of sexual discrimination. If trustee status is offered to male inmates, it also needs to be offered to female inmates as well.*

Now we were writing two kites every day. One for commissary and one advocating for equal rights as trustees.

Finally, the administrator walked into our pod. "Ms. Young, you're killing me." Dropping a six-inch stack of kites on the table, he continued, "I have to answer each one of these personally. I thought maybe I could wait you ladies out, but there's no stopping you! I don't have time in my day to answer these. What will it take?"

"It's simple. Add some healthier food choices to commissary, along with Chapstick, dental floss, and lotion. That's all we want. And let some of the women be trustees."

"I'll look into the commissary; I can do something about that, but I can't do anything about female trustees right now. The trustees live in a separate pod with additional privileges. I don't have room for a separate women's pod, and I can't mix men and women, but I will consider something for the future. Can you live with that?"

"Okay, that's fair. We'll wait to see what you come up with. No more kites—for now. I'll temporarily ground all kites."

As he left the pod, the women cheered. They were proud to be part of something that was making a positive change. Together, we were choosing our own empowerment.

A few weeks later, Wayne entered our pod carrying two large cardboard boxes. Dropping them on tables, he said, "These are the new food items I'm considering adding to the commissary. I'd like you women to try them and write a recommendation for the items you think we should include. I've also included a spreadsheet with the prices I will need to charge for each item. If the price is too high to be affordable, I want to know that too. I can't allow Q-tips or dental floss for security reasons, but I think there's a good assortment of items there. Knock yourselves out."

Hoots of delight filled the pod as the women attacked the boxes. "I want the Twizzlers!"

"I want the peanut butter."

"I want…"

"Stop!" Ruby called out. "Miss Toby made this happen for us. She gets to decide who gets what."

I looked at the gathered crowd, "I have an idea. We're going to open everything here and each one of us is going to try a sample and then tell me what you think. How does it taste? Would you buy it if it was on commissary at the marked price? I'll make a list and keep track of what we think. Let's rate each item from one to five. Everyone, go get your spoons."

The pod celebrated as we championed a cause. We were heard. The exhilaration was tangible; it sizzled through the pod with the aroma of victory and every woman wore a huge smile. These women, some for the first time, felt the power of standing up for themselves in a productive and resourceful way within a system they could not control. A lesson I hoped they would take with them out into the world, but, for now, there was peanut butter enough for everyone, and we binged!

Angie approached me with a closed fist. "There's one item here I don't think we can share. We'd like you to have it." Uncurling her fingers, a single tube of Chapstick lay in her hand.

I accepted.

7.

## AN EMPTY LOFT

**I HAD BEEN IN JAIL NOW** for two months. I'd smile at myself ironically when I remembered the fit I threw, thinking I'd be in jail for a short two weeks. It wasn't so bad. I was finding a place here.

It had been nine months since Dad's cancer diagnosis. He and Mom were both my staunch advocates and they worried most about my emotional health. Not only did they appear before the judge on my first day back in Kansas to petition for my thyroid medication, but they also requested additional visits.

"We have a very large family, and our daughter is in a precarious mental state. We respectfully request an additional two hours of family visits plus one hour a week for a spiritual visit from our family priest and a one-hour meeting with a counselor."

Jail policy allowed a thirty-minute visit once a week. But the judge compassionately approved their requests, and the jail was bound to honor his ruling.

Occasionally my brothers or sisters would visit, but my parents came regularly. Dad's health declined. Nearing his end, too determined for a wheelchair, but too weak to walk on his own, my sister helped him into the visiting room for his last visit with me. Sitting down, he dismissed her with a wave, "I've got this."

Drawn and withered, Dad held a vomit tray close. "Toby,

you've got a lot to face, and I won't be here to help you, but you can do this. Don't lose hope. Remember, we Phalens don't complain. We just buckle down and get through it."

I nodded, knowing our family motto by heart. *Phalens don't complain.*

"Oh, and one more thing. Rob doesn't deserve this. I want you to promise me on my death bed you'll do whatever it takes to repair your marriage. I love you, Toby. And I've got to go."

I could not control my tears, I agreed and then I begged through sobbing breaths, "Dad, when you get to heaven, watch over me and when you see Emily, tell her I love her."

Five days after Dad's visit, the entire family gathered around him. The only empty seat was mine. Leaving his love behind, Dad eased out of our world while telling jokes and reciting cowboy poetry. I grieved alone behind bars; bars withheld me from Dad's death and my life.

*Daddy centered us. Somehow, within me, in a deep quiet place even at my young age, I felt infinitely secure to be by him. My budding self-worth delicately germinated beneath the glow of his adoration.*

*Daddy worked the night shift at the railroad, but he gave his days to us. He sprinted chaotically, yanking on kite strings just in time to save each from disaster. We giggled hysterically at Daddy's cartoonish antics. Like a magnet, the ground pulled the kites down while Daddy's magic tugs set them free. My heart soared with them.*

*When Daddy played ping pong with our neighbor, his movements dazzled me. The little white ball flashed like lightning. I watched for hours. At bedtime, I'd fall asleep to the tiny white balls bouncing behind my closed eyes.*

*How can I live without you, Dad? How will any of us? You were the center of our world.*

A few days later, when we were all in our cells for the night, a call came over the speaker, "Young, pack your things, you're leaving."

"Where am I going?"

"Your attorney will be here to explain it to you."

Minutes later, Jim hustled into the meeting room. "Your brother bonded you out for your dad's funeral. It's just a forty-eight-hour bond, you'll be returning on Saturday, but your family wants you there with them. Your brother put his house up for collateral, so if you don't come back in forty-eight hours, his family will lose their home." Ironically, what Jim didn't know is that I held no regard for the financial risk, it was the rule that compelled me to return.

"Where would I go? Why would anyone think I wouldn't come back?"

"Well, you did run away once, Toby."

I acknowledged him with a shrug. "Touché. I'm not the same woman I was then, Jim."

My youngest brother and one of my sisters picked me up at four o'clock in the morning. The air felt fresher, the moon brighter, and I couldn't pull my face away from the car window and the marvel of early dawn.

My brother explained, "We wanted to avoid the media so we thought a late-night pickup would be good." *Surely, he's exaggerating. The media must have died down by now...*

My sister handed me an apple—a fruit I had been denied. I stared spellbound, longer than a moment, then took a bite with a loud crunch. I marveled at stars I hadn't seen in months. I couldn't believe how much I missed them! These were the same familiar streets I'd driven freely, but everything felt different. The world changed; or maybe it was me.

*Who am I? Sometimes I don't even recognize myself, but one thing is certain, I'll never take freedom for granted again.*

Dad left big shoes. We indecisively milled about my parents' house, uncertain of the simplest things. Like salt in our wounds, a local news station broadcast live, "From the steps of Blessed

Sacrament Church in KCK where Toby Young's father will be buried tomorrow." The media stoked the community's demand for my bloodied head. I stared at the television in disbelief where a montage of familiar images flashed... the Safe Harbor Prison Dog van, John Manard's mugshot, my dad in a press conference before my arrest, and of course, still photographs of me in black and white striped disgrace. I sensed my family's grim glare in the dead silence.

My sister mumbled into the air, loud enough to reach my ears, "See what you've done?" Then the barrage started: Voices joined in the choir of questions.

"You are news, Toby. Whatever you do makes the news. It's been a crazy three months."

*Yes, I know. I have a front-row seat to the crazy!*

"We had to put up no trespassing signs at the end of the driveway. Rob also had to. They mobbed Greg on his way to school."

"The phone rings constantly asking for someone to make a statement."

"Geraldo called the other day!"

"You can't imagine what you've put us all through. You don't know how hard this has been." With angry glares and pointing fingers, my sisters exploded into angry accusations.

I thought I'd assume my place in the family as the eldest child, but my siblings felt differently. My fall from grace had displaced my family's respect for me. With my position revoked I felt unready to fight for it, so I conceded. Siblings that I had fed, diapered, bathed, and sheltered from Daddy's tragic accident, usurped all mercy. I felt isolated in my family home. I began to suspect that whatever punishment I received from the system would do little to quell their outrage. For them, justice could never be served. They suffered humiliation from my mistakes.

My youngest sister offered, "Let's take a walk down to the

pond."

With my head down and tears dripping and relieved to get out of the wildcat den, I followed. There were seven siblings in our family, none closer to me than this sister.

"The family has decided that you will sit in the choir loft tomorrow at Dad's funeral. The media circus will create something less dignified than Dad deserves. His funeral should be about him, not you. We talked this over with Mom and she agrees. And don't bother her with this. She's too upset. Just do what she wants. We all think this is best."

Blindsided, I felt betrayed by this turn in our conversation. My whole world fell apart. My Shame Dragon reared its head with soulless eyes, venomous fangs, battle-worn scales, and talons striking me down. Her heavy tail spiked my heart.

I already experienced a mighty fall by going to jail. I thought I would retain the unconditional love, peace, and acceptance of my family—everything that had been shown to me by our parents behind the glass wall of the visiting room. Instead of the unconditional love I knew I needed in order to heal, the love I expected devolved into something conditional.

*If it isn't given here, where will I find a nurturing space again? Am I worthless? Is this the life I am doomed to live? Scurrying around in the shadows, never to be let into the embrace of unconditional love I thought would greet me?*

From deep inside I felt a tiny tickle, a slight nudge, and then a lioness roared in outrage, and I found the courage to rise and stand up for myself.

This is not who I am. I am still worthy. I am still the eldest. I am still here. *Daddy's eyes still held mine.*" I am not sitting in the choir loft. I can't believe any of you even thought I'd agree!"

"Toby, just wait and listen, you'll understand…"

Angrily I turned away. I felt a strong spirit rising as I marched toward the house, passing my brother, Tom.

I confronted him, "Are you in on this nonsense? I am NOT sitting in the choir loft."

Tom shook his head, "No, Toby, I never agreed to that. I'm on your side."

I drew strength from his support.

As I rushed into the house, Mom intercepted me, "Toby, are you okay? What's got you so upset?"

I paused, "I love you, Mom, but it seems my…" I raised my fingers, jabbing air quotes around my next word, "… *sisters* have decided I should sit in the choir loft at Dad's funeral tomorrow. Is this what *you* want?"

"I don't know what I want, Toby. Your sisters think it would be best."

My sister barged in behind me, "Toby, Rob and the boys don't want you there at all. In fact, Rob is threatening to not come if you are there. Sitting in the choir loft is a good compromise. After all, Dad was like a father to him."

"Well, he wasn't *like* a father to me. He *is* my father."

I yearned for the cocoon of my jail cell and pod mates who treated me with respect, "I won't stay here and make Dad's funeral any harder for you nor will I make it any easier for you to hate me. Take me back to jail." Jail humiliated me less, so I stood up for myself.

Voices continued at elevated pitches downstairs. I heard a car pull into the driveway and soon the bedroom door opened.

"Toby?" Jim walked in.

"I see they've called the cavalry. I'm sorry you've been drawn into this, Jim, but I'm glad you're here. Can you give me a ride back to the jail? I can be ready to go in five minutes."

"Toby don't be so hard on them. I thought you'd be coming from jail with an officer escort, handcuffed and shackled, so I volunteered to sit with you in the choir loft. It was my idea."

"Well, I'm not wearing handcuffs now am I Jim? And I'm not

sitting in the choir loft. Dumb idea."

Unable to sway me, Jim headed downstairs.

I knew what I had done. In hindsight, I knew what I'd done to everyone.

*What kind of sacrifice would absolve my sin in their eyes? I'm beginning to realize I may never know. No punishment would earn their forgiveness. I need to get out of here. How can I get back to the jail if no one will drive me there? It's much too far to walk. I wonder if I could call the police to come and get me? They take people to jail all the time, but do they do it by request? Seems kind of odd to call 911 and ask for a ride to jail...*

I heard lighter steps on the stairs, and Mom joined me on the bed. Holding my hand tightly, she said, "Toby, that was the dumbest idea I've ever heard. I can't believe they almost talked me into it. I want you next to me tomorrow in your place as the oldest. This is not your sisters' decision to make. And if Rob decides not to come, well that's his choice."

I knew exactly which two of my sisters had championed the choir loft idea, and which two followed along. My youngest brother didn't like to argue with the sisters. That left Tom and Mom in my corner. My heart surged with love for them in their willingness to stand up and take an unpopular position in such a difficult time. I was so sorry to bring more difficulty into this already unbearable day.

Starting to get an idea of the immense battle I faced within my own family, I knew I would have no home base from which to recharge. This would be a battle that killed the idea of regaining unconditional love, destroyed forgiveness, gutted grace, and murdered mercy. It would be a battle with no winners. Only heartache and wounded egos would remain.

My parents owned a large house, but our family was larger. With all beds taken, I searched for a place to sleep. Being the last to arrive, and now, evidently, the bottom of the pecking order, I had two options: the couch or the floor. I chose the couch, but Mom chose me.

"Toby, I have this huge bed and it's just me. Now it will be us—you and me."

She was my champion. We didn't sleep much but spent the night holding hands and sharing stories about Dad.

"Remember all our canoe trips? Dad always insisted everyone tip over. If we didn't, he'd jump out and rock our canoe until we did!" Mom said.

"Yep, I got wise to that pretty quick and just tipped mine over the minute we got in the water just to get it over with."

"And his garden! Your dad moved us to five different houses looking for the perfect garden!"

"Oh, how he loved it here with his one-acre garden plot and a pond to water it!"

"Remember that year he grew okra just because he never had—even knowing we all hated it?"

"Him, too! Dad wouldn't eat it either."

Mom and I howled with laughter.

"Remember that camping trip in Colorado when Dad took me to the little camp store one night on the back of his 100cc Honda motorcycle?"

"That deer ran out into the road and at the last minute jumped over you guys!"

"His feet brushed my helmet." I loved to reminisce with Mom. "How about that trip to Chicago for Thanksgiving? The icy highway closed so we never got off the interstate since we wouldn't be allowed back on. Dad drove with one set of wheels off the side of the road to keep traction."

Mom's eyes drifted to the ceiling as if exploring a scene in her mind. "It was so freezing cold! We were all bundled into our sleeping bags, heater running full blast, and still shivering."

I added, "Aunt Martha was stunned to see us, but what a fun

time we had! We were so cold we couldn't sleep so we sang songs the whole way. And Grandma was with us."

"And your college roommate who couldn't get home for Thanksgiving because of the blizzard, so we just took her with us right out into that blizzard!"

Towards dawn, we drifted into a warm sleep, still holding hands.

My dad's death and his funeral coerced a turning point in my life. Even without my looming sentencing, our family was adrift. My sisters tried to take charge, bullying their way through the family.

Furious that I had somehow swayed Mom into letting me sit next to her, they found ways to shame me. Their relentless punishment finally found the perfect weapons, my sons.

"Rob and the boys are here. They're on the right side of the church. You're not to look at them."

*My boys! My boys! How can I not look at them? My thoughts in jail were constantly of them. Their faces filled my dreams. Their voices called to me all day long. I ached to hold them, talk with them, hug them, and tell them everything would be okay, that we would get through this, like Mom and Dad used to do for me.*

"If you so much as glance at them, they will leave and that would be selfish of you."

I didn't look, but I should have.

Today, I know that our world would have been very different if I had listened to my gut and made my way over there to hug them. I believe this is what they expected, but I let others bully my gaze and kept my head down. I've lamented my squashed courage ever since.

Father Al, who had been visiting me weekly at the jail, approached us. "So, you want six gifts at the back of the church for the offering?"

"Wait a minute. Six?" I immediately locked my eyes on my

sister while she defiantly returned my gaze for a moment before dropping her eyes to the floor. Although I continued to stare at my sister, Father Al expected my next words, "There are seven of us. We'll need seven items for the offering, please."

Father Al nodded at me as a smile touched his face. I realized he timed his question perfectly to give me an opportunity to be included. My heart brimmed with love for this priest who navigated a treacherous road within my family dynamics. "I'll have seven items at the back."

At dinner after the funeral Rob and Greg did not appear, but Eric did. My youngest sister parked herself in a chair next to him, guarding him from my approach, and, once again, I let her.

Years later, another sister would accuse me of not caring enough and shared with me that all Eric wanted that day was to talk to me. My heart wanted to stop beating. I ached to be his mom again.

My sister did her best to protect him, and she thought she did it out of love. But if she understood love, she would have paved a compassionate path for us to reunite.

"He couldn't take his eyes off you." I reminded her of our sister who had assumed the role of Eric's watchdog, blocking him from me at every opportunity. She brushed it away as inconsequential to avoid responsibility, but the consequences held tremendous pain. I didn't know at the time that it would be the last chance I'd ever have with my sons.

"I don't know why a mother would not talk to her own son," she reiterated.

*There is another that has the power to heal the fractures between me and my family. My sisters could have nurtured the opportunity, but they chose to fuel guilt. My adult sons had the opportunity to forgive me and love me, despite my transgressions. Much of my family showed animosity toward me. Meanwhile, I couldn't yet see the bigger picture, and at that time I failed to forgive them and love them anyway. The same obstacles that prevented them from accepting me, prevented me from understanding them.*

# 8.

## THE BOX DIDN'T FIT

**SATURDAY ROLLED AROUND AND** my forty-eight-hour bond ended. A few days ago, I dreaded this moment, sure that the required return to jail would be devastating after a breath of freedom. But two days commandeered by my sisters made me eager to return to the monotony and safe routine of my jail cell. No underhanded surprises awaited me there.

Thankful for the pivotal point toward healing with Tom and Mom, I could move forward. They gave me courage for the long road ahead. Based on their support, love, and desire to forgive, I knew they would always be there for me.

*But Jim was right, way too much drama out here.* I knew then that it wasn't the media that dogged my days, my sisters stoked the drama. If I were relentlessly faced with their heavy-handed influence against me, their heightened emotions and frequent slights would wear me down in no time. I knew I wasn't strong enough to face that yet.

I had the opportunity to say my last goodbye to Dad. I felt his arms around me and could hear his words, "We'll get through this too." At peace, I realized the time had come to get back to the reality of facing my future.

The justice system uses a sentencing grid, a spreadsheet I

suppose, although this grid was in use long before spreadsheets became so common. The severity of a crime receives a numerical rating represented in rows while the defendant's criminal history gets an alphabetical rating represented in columns. The intersection of the column and row is the "box" a case falls into. That box determines the appropriate, non-biased sentence recommendation of presumptive probation or presumptive imprisonment and the range of months.

There is a unique gray area called Border Boxes. Cases that fall into a border box usually default to presumptive probation but are sentenced at a judge's discretion. With no criminal record at all, not even a traffic ticket, I fell into a border box. I believed that would be my saving grace.

Jim approached me with a plea deal. "Toby, I know you're in the border box and should be given probation, but I've been talking to the prosecutor. He says he can't agree to probation because the media would crucify him. It looks like you're going to have to do some time."

"How can the media hold any influence on our legal system? It doesn't make sense!"

Nevertheless, the media wields the power to pressure prosecutors—who are elected to office—by swaying public opinion. My case was a big one, and the media insisted on my blood. Border box be damned, the public wanted prison time.

Going to trial would mean days of sitting in a courtroom while the media salivated for a story, my face plastered on every news channel in every living room across the country. I didn't want any part of that circus. Weighing my options, a plea deal, even if it meant time in prison, seemed to be the better choice. I'd done several months already, I could do a few more.

"Okay, Jim. I think I can do the time. What are we talking about? I've already been in jail four months. A couple more, you think?"

"No, Toby. We're looking at more time than that. He wants twenty-one months."

"TWENTY-ONE MONTHS! Jim, I can NOT do twenty-one months. That's almost two years!"

Jim waited until I took a breath. "Yes, you can, Toby. I think you can do it. Twenty-one months will fly by."

"It won't fly by, Jim. Nothing *flies by* in here. Time drags along in slow motion when you're locked up."

Jim waited with a pragmatic stare. I processed my options. I stared at the floor. I glanced at Jim. I watched seconds tick by on the wall clock. I counted as if to prove the dragging of time behind bars, but a minute was still a minute.

I sighed. I stared at the floor. Two more minutes passed.

Finally, I took the lesser of two evils. At least it was another step forward and moving forward meant this journey had an end. "Okay Jim, make the deal."

# 9.

## I'm Already Gone

**SITTING IN THE POD**, pondering my looming twenty-one-month sentence, I struggled to remain optimistic. Angie and Vicky were trying their best to raise my spirits, when suddenly the pod door opened, and Jessica walked in. Delighted to see my old roommate, I jumped up and ran to hug her.

"Jessica! How are you doing? Are you okay? Did they get your meds straightened out?"

"I'm good Toby. I'm on my meds and the voices are gone."

I ran up the stairs, opened the box under my bunk, and returned to Jessica, presenting her the items I'd been guarding. "You saved all these for me?" Jessica's incredulous grin filled her face.

"Well, of course I did. I said I would, didn't I? And I added two noodles and another candy bar. Welcome back! Best of all, I have an empty bunk in my room, Jessica. You can stay with me."

The intercom interrupted our celebration, "Young, you have an attorney visit."

Jim waited with some surprising news. "The prosecutor has accepted your plea. All we must do is go before the judge to confirm it. You were scheduled to do that the day after tomorrow, but the judge has fifteen minutes free right now. If you're willing, we can go and trick the media, who are expecting it to be in two days."

I laughed out loud. "You know I'd love an opportunity to trick those hounds! Let's go."

Quickly ushered into a gloriously empty courtroom, I agreed to the deal and hustled back to my pod where Jessica waited. An hour later we were again interrupted by a familiar call. "Young, you have an attorney visit."

This time Jim had even better news. Impressed with my return to jail after the funeral bond, the bail bondsman offered to apply the $2,000 cash previously paid and the house collateral to another, longer bond.

"You're going home, Toby, for forty days. Your sentencing is scheduled for July twelfth, but you'll be released on bond today. Your brother is on his way to pick you up now."

Speechless, I never expected to go home at all.

Jim continued, "Officially, they grant this so you can 'get your affairs in order.' It would be a good time to go to the dentist, get a checkup from your doctor—I don't know what the medical care is like in Topeka Correctional Facility, so you might as well go in prepared. Your mother is over the moon and can't wait for you to get home. Go pack your stuff."

Even in my excitement, I had doubts.

*The funeral certainly wasn't easy. Could I handle more time with the sisters? The media? Am I strong enough? Maybe I should just decline and hang out here. No, I need to spend time with Mom. Going to the medical appointments made sense, but what I really needed was to stock up on hugs. I knew there'd be no amount of hugging loved ones that would make me miss them less when I was gone…*

* * *

Being home brought pure delight, and my spirit soared.

Mom and I planned a trip to the country to visit her cousin and stop in to spend a couple of days with Kerry, a good friend of mine.

Delighted to see us, Kerry shared with me, "Toby, the marshals came here looking for you. Rob told them you liked to come here and stay to relax. They asked if I'd seen you. I told them no, but I was rooting for you Toby. I'm glad I didn't know where you were because I don't know if I could have turned you in. Every few days, they'd call and say, 'any news?' and I thought if that's the best they got, they'll never find you."

I carried a packet of letters from John that I kept hidden and read every night before I fell asleep. Somehow, John discovered that I was out on bond and managed to send letters to me. He begged me to write back, and I did, but I shouldn't have.

I hung out with Mom and Tom and my days were filled with joy, peace, and hope for a future not too distant.

One day, a cloud of gravel dust swirled behind Rob's truck as he drove down my parents' quarter-mile driveway. We had not spoken at all. I tried to call him after Dad's last visit, but he never accepted my calls. Letters went unanswered, and I just stopped trying.

I choked at the coming confrontation and the expected litany of Rob's rants. Running upstairs, I wedged myself under the bed like a five-year-old.

Puzzled, Mom followed. "Toby! What's wrong with you? Don't be ridiculous. Just come downstairs and talk to Rob. What are you running from?"

Rob and I sat on the porch while Mom stayed in the shadows of the open dining room window. It took twenty-eight years in a dead marriage and an escape from prison to force a real conversation between us.

Rob's posture, expression, and breathing conveyed his

belligerence; countless one-sided conversations proved my insignificance throughout our time together.

*How is it possible that we shared three decades void of candor? I can't play this game any longer.*

There on the porch, his face flushed red from anger and his hands clenched with tension. Rob knew exactly how to cut me to the quick. His eyes and demeanor gave him away, and I imagined the words, "I'm here to take your sons from you," but other words fell out.

"You owe me a fucking apology."

I blinked at his use of my new favorite word; one I had never heard him say. Rob hadn't driven all the way down here, with trash bags of my clothes in the back of his truck, for an apology.

Annoyed, I asked, "An apology? What do you really want Rob?"

His eyes bulged and spittle flew from his mouth as he yelled, "Do you have any idea what you and the media have done to me? You have RUINED my life. I can't even go out in public! People look at me and I know what they're thinking, 'What must be wrong with him that she would leave him for a convicted murderer?' You owe me a fucking apology for the way the media has treated me!"

"The media? You've got to be kidding. I can't control the media. They've been chasing me around too! Did you see those photos in Tennessee? Maybe the media should apologize to ALL of us—me most of all!"

We yelled and shouted over each other. Neither hearing the other.

Surprised that I defended myself—something new in our relationship—Rob shouted, "Are you raising your voice to me? How DARE you raise your voice! YOU," pushing his finger into my arm and poking with each word, "HAVE RUINED MY LIFE.

Ruined it. My life is OVER! You don't have the right to raise your voice to me. Our boys are a mess, and YOU (finger stab) NEED (finger poke) TO FIX (poke poke) THEM (stab stab stab)."

"Well then, maybe you should tell them they have YOUR permission to talk to me since you're the one who told them they had to choose between us."

"Never!"

We sat there in silence for a few minutes when Rob added, almost as an afterthought, "What about us?"

"Us?"

*There is no us. Maybe there never was…*

I whispered, "I'm already gone, Rob. Can't you see that? I left. I'm already gone."

Rob stood and faced me. I remained seated. He struggled to control himself and said, "I'll call an attorney." Then, uncharacteristically, he leaned over, kissed the top of my head, and walked away. Stunned and relieved, I had expected much worse.

*I think he knew we were already over. Maybe he's as relieved as I am. I don't think I was a great wife for him. I gave up on us a long time before, but he had no idea how far I had gone.*

As Rob tossed bags of clothes from the back of his truck, I stood tall with steel in my eyes, the wind blowing my hair and my arms crossed. Rob made no eye contact, he marched to the door of the truck, almost triumphantly, yanked the handle, jumped in, and sped off down the road.

Rob's truck boiled off dust while my mind perused the image of John's final text, just before the escape, "Good morning Baby. I love you."

When confronted, I told Rob, "Wrong number." Rob couldn't be bothered; he couldn't miss hunting with his buddies.

He responded, "You're not sexually capable of having an

affair anyway," and he left that day too.

As Rob's truck disappeared, I wondered why he didn't love me.

Mom walked out and embraced me on the porch. "I had no idea, Toby. No idea how he'd been treating you. I know your dad asked you to promise to fix things, but if he had witnessed what I just did, he'd change his mind. I'm speaking for both of us and rescinding his request. You can forget about your promise to Dad. You can't fix this marriage."

Rob filed for an emergency divorce. He phoned a few times to finalize the details. Ironically, those conversations were the most civil ones we'd ever had. His first offer took everything 'because of my actions.' I rejected that. I'd made two-thirds of our income during most of our marriage.

Eventually, I wore down. I agreed to let him have the house in return for a conservative amount of equity, to be paid out when I was released from prison. I relinquished my right to half of his retirement and savings. The settlement wasn't enough, and my attorney advised against it, but I just wanted to untangle this last knot and move on.

I held firm on one thing, though. Rob insisted I change my name back to Phalen, but I refused. I'd already slandered the name *Young*, I planned to keep that one through my prison journey and change it back to Phalen with my release and a fresh start.

Another memory danced through my mind. The night before the escape, I sat at my desk finishing my last weekly newsletter for Safe Harbor Prison Dog Program. Rob headed up the steps for bed and called down, "Good night."

I looked up at him and replied, "Goodbye." My heart dropped at this slip of the tongue, worried he'd come down to confront me. All our plans would be out the window if Rob caught an inkling of deceit, but he just turned away and headed up the stairs and out of my life.

Rushing through a divorce before going to prison did me no good. Legally, any divorce requires a stable mind and due diligence, I gave away too much but I took freedom. Urgently pushed through the court system, our divorce was finalized July eleventh, the day before my sentencing, five months to the day from our escape.

# 10.

## THE OPEN DOOR HAS BARS

**MOM AND I HAD ENJOYED** our trip to the country and our weeks together. I completed the necessary doctor and dentist visits and even got a new pair of glasses to replace the ones smashed in the crash.

Rob refused to pay for my glasses, but my friend Steve stepped up and covered them for me.

I didn't see much media around and felt relief for that blessing. One reporter from a local news station called me several times, offering to tell my side of the story. I politely declined. The day before my return to jail, I received one last, desperate call. "Toby, you're running out of time. I can have a crew at your mom's house in thirty minutes if you just say the word."

"No, I don't think I have anything to say."

"If you don't talk to me and give me your side of the story, I'll have no choice but to give a scandalous report on tonight's news."

"Now, I'm really not interested."

True to her word, I watched her report. "Tomorrow, Toby Young will be in court to learn her sentence for helping her convicted murderer-lover escape from prison." The words *convicted murderer-lover* dripped with disdain and disbelief that a highly esteemed woman in our society could stoop to such an act and implied, surely, that whatever sentence she receives is well-deserved.

I relished and rued the day. Although my sisters had mostly stayed away during my time out on bond, everyone decided to make an appearance for the court date. After all, the world would be watching, and my sisters valued our public image more than anything. We needed to look like a family united.

Two sisters drove in from out of town. The rest of my siblings lived nearby. Mom fixed a big lunch, almost like we were having a holiday. I didn't eat.

Mom requested a family photo in front of the house. I obliged but wondered why we were marking this day as one of significance.

I had not seen nor talked to my sons during my time off, but not because I didn't try.

I spent a lot of time selecting an outfit for my court appearance. I wanted the media to finally have a decent photo of me. Although they only used it once, from then on they preferred to use the black and white stripes as often as they could.

The Leavenworth County Courthouse, twenty minutes away, beckoned. Six siblings and my mom came with me to the courthouse, but I faced my prison time alone.

I wanted to cry during the ride, but, at the same time, I was ready to cross another threshold in this journey. The more steps forward I took, the sooner I'd be done with this nightmare.

It was time for me to leave the relative quiet of jail and head into the unknown of the Topeka Correctional Facility (TCF), part of the Kansas Department of Corrections (KDOC)—the same entity from which I helped an inmate escape. I found it ironic that KDOC, technically my victim, now held the key to my confinement.

For the first time, I would enter the courthouse through the front door. Accustomed to the clamoring melee of media, I brushed through the reporters lining the sidewalk. They tried to block my path, standing directly in front of me in the middle of the sidewalk thrusting microphones in my face.

"Toby, how does it feel knowing you are going to prison?"

*What a stupid question! How do you think it feels, jerk!*

I spoke not a word. Beyond my naivety, I distrusted all media snakes who sensationalized every story regardless of the cost. They often took bits and pieces to fabricate a slanted view. The media honored not the human condition nor truth, therefore I remained silent.

In the packed courtroom, I could hear the clock ticking over the reporters clamoring around, cameras in position.

"I wish they would just hurry up and get this started. I want to get it over with."

Mom held my hand tightly, "Toby, why would you want to rush through these last minutes?"

I squeezed back. "Mom, I'm ready to move forward. The end isn't in this courtroom. This is just the beginning. And being in this room with the media isn't where I want to be. A step forward is a step closer to being done with this."

I hugged her one last time as Jim motioned for me to join him. The judge kept it short and sweet, "Ms. Young, I've accepted your plea and sentence you to twenty-one months in the state prison." Officers were poised to handcuff me and lead me through the side door into my warren. I didn't look back.

I forgot they take the shoes of inmates away in the holding area. When I dressed for court in my bright summer skirt and lime green sweater with flats, socks didn't seem appropriate. But now, I wished I had considered my options more carefully as I sat for hours, barefoot in the filthy holding cell.

I wasn't taken upstairs until just before evening lockdown. Jessica smiled broadly; her whole face wrinkled with joy. "We've been watching you on TV today. You sure gave those reporters the brush off!"

Ruby added, "If looks could kill, Miss Toby, you'd be doing a longer sentence."

"That mutherfucker think he big to try an' get you to talk wit' him."

They all hollered at once. I couldn't understand anything through their clutter of words.

They laughed. Some of the faces were new, but I felt loved. To them, I was a celebrity, but as soon as it began, it was over. An officer appeared for lockdown and the chatter dissolved like two drops of water on a hot skillet, hopping around for a short second before hissing away.

Placed in a cell alone, I cried. My world caved in around me.

*Alone and unwanted by some of the people who meant the most to me in the whole world. Will that ever change? But tomorrow, tomorrow will be a new day and I will be surrounded by women I know, women who are family to me.*

I couldn't wait for morning. I had so much to catch up on.

At six o'clock, long before the pod opened, the call came over the speaker. "Young, pack your things. You're being moved." Again, without goodbyes, I processed out of the Leavenworth County Jail. It all made sense. They'd kept me in holding until lockdown and were moving me out before breakfast. They didn't want me riling up the other inmates.

An hour away, I dreaded my arrival at TCF. Several months before, I accompanied some of the unit team leaders from Lansing to take a tour of TCF's dog program and compare it to my own Safe Harbor Prison Dog Program at the Lansing Correctional Facility for men. I had been observed by TCF's inmate dog handlers as someone to be admired. I'd met with TCF's unit team leaders as peers.

*Now, I was as arriving as an inmate, and I shrunk with embarrassment. Why did it have to be TCF we had toured that day?*

*This whole thing would be much easier if no one knew who I was and how far I'd fallen from all good grace.*

As newly arrived State Inmate 86519, I kept my eyes down. Adding insult to injury, I was told in no uncertain terms that I would not be considered for the dog program. In fact, I wasn't even allowed to pet the dogs.

There are three levels of security or custody in the prison system. Minimum security inmates are not considered a risk and are often housed in units without fencing. They are allowed jobs outside the prison and often wear regular clothes. This is the classification every inmate wishes for. Medium security inmates are contained behind fences, but they have unlimited access to the yard and library and other activities. They also have access to many prison jobs.

Inmates dread maximum security. Kept locked in their pods most of the day and provided the yard for one hour at a specific time, they are allowed the library and some meetings, but approved passes were required to be out of the unit.

Two weeks after I'd arrived, I attended a meeting to determine my classification. I had no illusions of minimum custody, but I hoped for medium. "Ms. Young, you have an exception placed on you by the Secretary of Corrections for the State of Kansas. It reads as follows: Ms. Young is mandated to be classified as maximum security. This mandate is for a ten-year period and cannot be appealed."

"Ten years! But my sentence is only twenty-one months."

"Obviously, we can't keep you longer than your sentence, but if you should re-offend for any reason, the mandate will be in place, and you will automatically be considered maximum custody for whatever new crimes you might commit."

"I won't be back," I said resolutely. I wouldn't give them the satisfaction.

I reached a new depth of shame; unlike the streets from which others came, I swan dived from a golden pedestal of status into this hellish sewer. Was I more aware of the treatment because I hadn't come from the streets? Did my own experiences punctuate the system that everyone knew to be flawed, biased, and downright ugly?

As a volunteer, I knew the men's prison and how it worked. Some cowered away from a glare. Loyalty could not be broken out of fear of violent retaliation.

I remembered one of my most promising dog handlers who took a drug rap for another more powerful inmate—an inmate who later beat his dog to death during a drug-induced rage. No one had the courage to stop it.

Invisible to the untrained eye, undercurrents of unspeakable power forced inmates to submit or pay the price. Men's prison is psychological warfare with tangible consequences. Probably because it oozes adolescent testosterone with no healthy outlet. A boiling caldron, the entire place could be touched off with the slightest spark.

What would the women's prison be like? I expected the same turmoil.

What I encountered instead was disorganized and chaotic. It was more akin to high school than a life-threatening power regime. In fact, in comparison to the tensions in the men's prison, women's prison bored me. It was an endless loop of drama.

"Shelby was looking at Mary! I'm going to get her in the showers." A weak threat since no one ever *got* anyone in the showers, at least while I was there.

There were some fights, but they smoldered slowly before erupting and then burned out quickly. Once, my next-door neighbor's girlfriend thought I was trying to steal the love of her life. The girlfriend, who weighed close to 450 pounds, declared in the dayroom, "I'm going to get you, Young."

Women scurried over to warn me. I laughed. "I'm not

interested in anybody's girlfriend, and if she wants to *get* me, come on because she'll have to catch me; and I don't see that happening."

Some with unearned authority controlled the television in the dayroom. No discussion. If you wanted to watch something, you needed to ask a favor of the woman who *owned* the TV. Of course, nobody in prison *owned* anything; it was a status given by other, weaker inmates, kissing up to someone they thought had power. I never bothered watching anything at all as I filtered out "Who's the Daddy?" on the *Maury Povich Show*. The inmates acted surprised at the results every time, but it was the same thing over and over and over again. The drama broadcast from the TV mirrored the adolescent dramas of the dayroom.

The seating order on the benches in front of the TVs was also predetermined. Even if the spaces were empty, no one dared sit in a spot that *belonged* to someone. There were two TVs, one at each end of the U-shaped dayroom which created two power groups. In the center was "the bubble"—the control center from which officers observed the pod and popped doors to cells.

A single officer sat at a desk inside the pod directly in front of the bubble. With benches bolted to the concrete floor in front of the TVs, the rest of the space was filled with metal tables and stools also fastened to the floor. I spent most of my time in the dayroom sitting at one of the tables piecing together a jigsaw puzzle. Occasionally some of the women would drift by and ask, "What are you doing?"

"Working a puzzle."

"Why?"

"Something to do."

"Do you like doing that? I don't get puzzles."

*What is there to get?*

"They're actually pretty fun. Here you try a piece." Handing them a piece I'd already identified, I pointed out its place in the puzzle.

"Well, look at that! It fits. I did it."

Inevitably, they'd wander away, back to the mindlessness of *Maury* and the gang who captured their attention for hours. I didn't miss their company.

Cells surrounded the dayroom two tiers high. The lower tier cells provided bunk beds to accommodate two inmates. Two sets of stairs accessed single-person cells along the upper tier via a catwalk that circled the dayroom. Those coveted cells housed long standing inmates with good behavior, inmates with important jobs, or, in my case, inmates that Mental Health deemed vulnerable to cellmate manipulation.

TCF paid one psychologist for 750 inmates—lost souls—and we all needed counseling. I wondered how one person kept all our stories straight. It must have been an overwhelming and stressful job.

The best part of TCF were the in-person visits. No more bulletproof glass cruelly preventing my mother's touch, we could hold hands! Mom drove to visit me every Saturday. Occasionally, she'd come back on Sundays as well.

She brought the world to me. For the first time in my life, I held her undivided attention. Her presence alone filled my soul, and while we were together, the world was right. She brought a smile to my face until my cheeks hurt. I loved her so much for being with me and me alone.

With pockets stuffed full of quarters, she made it seem like she was having the time of her life, and there was no place else she'd rather be.

"Toby, you want another soda. Let's get some candy and chips."

Binging while we played Uno or Skip-Bo, we laughed as the prison walls around us disappeared. We were allowed to hug each other at the beginning and end of our visits but could hold hands as much as we wanted. We learned to play cards without letting go. Within the seven-hour visiting period, Mom's visits were the highlight of my week.

"Toby, this seems a lot better than jail. The visiting room is so nice and comfortable, compared to the booths lined with glass walls and talking through telephone receivers."

"It is better, Mom. We have a library, church, and time out in the yard every day. I just learned there's a book club! One of the women in my pod is going to get me fast-tracked into the club; it usually takes a month to get a space."

Mom never lost faith. She loved me through my poor choices, and I drew from her unwavering strength and unconditional love. Mom's visits got me through the dull and lengthy weeks. Many inmates never had this opportunity.

While the visiting room in the men's prison filled with wives and girlfriends, I quickly learned that women in prison don't get visits from husbands, boyfriends, or any men in their lives. The men just couldn't be bothered.

The isolation cultivated a shame that destroyed the self-esteem of anyone without external love—the most common challenge to inmates' mental health. Inmates needed someone to care for them and love them during their time. It became the divide between life and death.

Shame is the foundation of our criminal justice system. Strip searches, isolation, and confinement demean inmates beyond punishment. It is an industry built on degradation, intimidation, and dehumanization of people who have been caught and punished for life-altering mistakes.

It's difficult to make it through our justice system without feeling less than human. We all hoped for a lifeline or two, but it's up to each inmate to find the strength to grab hold and pull themselves up to survive.

My Shame Dragon grew into the space I provided, leaving no

room for hope; this dragon I had to slay. And I had the time. I began to dig into old wounds, and as I worked to discard misconceptions, my confidence emerged. Self-worth became my sword, and there, in TCF, I began the crusade to slay my Shame Dragon.

Father Al told me a story once about a tree growing in the middle of a sidewalk. "All it needed was a tiny crack for the seed to germinate. That seed sprouted after rain and sent down roots to establish a stronghold and secure a good foundation. Before long, the sprout pushed up through the crack, reaching for the sky to become a tree. If you must push through concrete, well then, you push concrete."

My dad would have loved that story.

Slaying shame is pushing concrete, reaching for the sky—for a new life—even when others would say there's no hope. Reach anyway, believe in the strength of the roots you've grown. We are all stronger than we give ourselves credit for.

After a couple of months in prison, I started to settle in and acclimate to the routine. I spent my days journaling and reading, and evenings piecing together a jigsaw puzzle in the dayroom, keeping mostly to myself.

One evening, laying out edge pieces, inmates started yelling, "Miss Toby, you're on TV again!"

I looked up. "… federally indicted," the reporter said. Staring in shock at my black and white striped image on the screen, my mind raced.

*Federally indicted. What does that mean, more court, more prison time? I have just become comfortable. Will this nightmare never end?*

My heart raced and I struggled to maintain control. Finally, I gave up and sank to a bench putting my head between my knees. I couldn't breathe.

Always drawn to drama, my fellow inmates called for an officer.

"She wus jus' on TV, and now she's havin' a heart attack!"

At the prison clinic, a nurse, concerned about my heart rate, talked on the phone requesting an ambulance when the prison psychologist walked in. "Ms. Young, I think you're having a panic attack. What happened today?"

"The news. I've been federally indicted. I don't even know what that means!"

"Ms. Young, you need to calm down. We'll get some answers for you."

He turned a crooked lip to the nurse, in a low tone, "Keep her up here for an hour or so and when she's calm, send her back to her unit." His lack of concern convinced me that I was fine.

Back on track, I asked to return to my pod where I immediately called my attorney, Jim. He didn't know any more than I did. "Toby, I just saw it on the news. It's Friday, not much I can do now. I'll get some answers for you on Monday. We'll figure it out. Try not to worry."

The Feds, thinking justice had not been properly served on the state side, decided to file federal charges of providing a gun to a felon. This meant a transfer of custody from the State of Kansas to the Federal Bureau of Prisons under the jurisdiction of the U.S. Marshals. And it meant another journey through another court system to receive another prison sentence.

*The guns. Those stupid guns. The dumbest part of this whole escape.*

Several months before my relationship with John became intimate, we had an innocent conversation in a group of dog handlers. Somehow, I casually mentioned that my husband loved guns, but I hated them. Even knowing that, he had gifted me with a pair of handguns. I didn't even know what kind they were, but they were obviously Rob's attempt to find some common ground.

"I thought this could keep you safe on the nights that I'm at the fire station," he reasoned.

"I hate guns. I would never shoot anybody," I countered.

"Well, some of the firefighters' wives are going to a shooting club. I thought you might like to go too."

I never took them out of their case, let alone out of the closet.

During the weeks before the escape, John dredged up our casual conversation and latched on to the idea of bringing those guns with us. "I won't ever use them, Toby, but we're going to be carrying a lot of cash with us and someone's going to see it and want to take it."

"Rob bought them. I can't just take them."

"He gave them to you, Toby. They're your guns. You have every right to bring them with you."

"I don't like guns, John. I don't want them with us."

"Come on, Baby. It will be okay. We might need them, just to keep our cash safe. I promise you I would never use them."

Day after day after day, this conversation repeated itself, and I finally relented. Now, those damned guns were back in my life. Fragments of my resurrected faith felt like they were being scattered in the winds of uncertainty and imminent defeat.

On a Friday afternoon, less than a week after the news, I walked into the pod after lunch, "Young, pack up. You're leaving."

My heart squeezed and writhed like a python swallowing a goat. Finding my way through my fear, I knew I was having a panic attack. I bypassed the medical clinic and headed for the unit team's office.

She was kind. "Toby, the U.S. Marshals are on their way. I can't tell you where you're going. In fact, I don't even know."

I trembled but fought back to stoicism, "How will my mom be able to find me? What if nobody knows where I am?"

With a hint of pity in her voice, she said, "Toby, there's a private prison in Leavenworth. Usually that's where federal prisoners are taken to await sentencing."

"Leavenworth?" I brightened. "That's closer to home. Maybe

it will be easier for Mom—I worry about her making the drive here every weekend." *Maybe this won't be so bad after all.*

I packed my belongings—long johns, a sweatshirt, toothbrush, toothpaste, a hairbrush, stamps and envelopes, colored pencils, and a Bible. Into the box went all the cards and letters I'd received. This box would wait for me on a shelf until I returned.

Allowed to take my glasses and the clothes on my back only, the marshals escorted me into an unmarked sedan. We rolled through the gates.

*Not my first prison departure, nor my grandest.*

Leaning my head against the car window, I watched the world pass by as I returned to that February morning. It was cold, oh so cold...

*God sent an icy wind, sharper than razor wire; it cut through the prison yard, stung the waiting visitors, and sapped the guards' resolve. A perfect day for a perfect plan.*

*I always looked forward to coming to the prison, but today, different emotions sizzled: apprehension, excitement, perhaps a bit of fear. So many things could go wrong, and few could go right.*

*I remembered how the prison looked the first day I came, eighteen months before. The imposing stone walls warned visitors to approach with caution. The massive Civil War-era buildings with iron-barred windows proclaimed, "danger lurks here." Tall fences topped with sharp barbed coils skirted the menacing fortress, separating "them" from "us."*

*I'd come to see the prison with different eyes. I knew these men inside. It didn't frighten me anymore. In fact, it almost seemed like home. I'd spent more hours here than under my own roof. Even so, today brought a different perspective. Whatever happened next, I would not be coming back here again. I would not be welcome. Doubt percolated. Did I really want to throw this all away? Was I going to miss it?*

*Be calm, Toby. It's just another adoption day.*

*I followed the gravel road around the perimeter of the fences. Visitor parking was available along this road; visitors would have to cover the rest of the distance on foot, but I was special. I could drive through the series of three gates and load dogs, under the watchful eyes of prison staff, to prepare for an adoption day. I'd done it hundreds of times before. There were only two people who knew this day would be different from the rest.*

*I waited for the outermost gate to open electronically via the command center located deep within the prison. Excitement and fear spiked my adrenaline. Conflict raged within me.*

*What am I doing here? Calm down, Toby...*

*Logic told me to run, but my heart yearned. Dozens of chances to say no came and went in the past few weeks, but I simply couldn't refuse. Soaring highs and lows had stolen both my sleep and my reason.*

*I firmly pressed the brake. In the small space between gates two and three, I shifted into park and killed the engine. Putting the keys in my pocket, I took a deep breath. This is it, Toby. You can do it! Closing the van door, I walked into the guard shack. My stomach twisted like tangled worms. My mouth, dry as a powder keg.*

*Just beyond gate three, in the vast area of the prison yard, dog handlers in cheap prison coats waited for me impatiently, stomping their feet, breath vaporizing in the frigid air. Red stocking hats blazed in a drab landscape while dogs danced on leashes.*

*I wondered, "Why red hats in such a drab setting?"*

*John had answered, "If the shooting starts, the guard towers have something to aim for."*

*I never saw red stocking hats the same again.*

*As I kept my handlers waiting, I reflected on these men I'd come to know well. They didn't exist to the outside community. These men without names, reduced to a number in a list of other numbers, stripped of human rights and dignity by an uncaring system, were no longer a part of our communities nor our consciousness. Mostly uneducated and unemployable, these disadvantaged men provided more value as inmates than as citizens.*

*Outside, the world gave them neither second thoughts nor second chances. I'd learned their names and their life stories. I'd listened. I looked and truly saw these men. Brennon, Safe Harbor's first dog handler of Darcy the pregnant setter, stood with a few others behind the gate waiting. To me, these men mattered. They weren't just numbers and records. Yet, I couldn't risk goodbyes.*

*I dreamed of changing the world, and I loved my creation where seven dogs had grown to almost a thousand. A limitless revolving queue of rescue dogs neutralized the acrid tones of prison, garnered national attention, and made a difference in our community, as well as the hearts and minds of those involved in the project.*

*That should have been enough. Why wasn't it? Why couldn't I just stay there and be the Dog Lady?*

"Ms. Young, we've arrived at CCA."

I had no idea what the future would bring, where I was going or when I'd be back. I simply took another step in this endless journey, but this time into a deep dark forest of uncertainty and dread.

# 11.

## Faith in Unlikely Places

CORRECTIONS CORPORATION OF AMERICA (CCA) owned and operated the Leavenworth Detention Center, my home during the federal proceedings against me. This maximum security, private, for-profit prison operated like a jail but also a business. Because CCA merely held the accused, it offered none of the perks of state prisons or federal penitentiaries each of which housed the convicted. CCA limited all luxuries and most necessities, as shareholders required. With a watchful eye on the bottom line, nobody objected to corners cut, such as substandard food, shorter visits, fewer privileges, and rough-shod medical care.

Once processed, an officer took me down another long hallway. I could hear women laughing and, despite my fear, I looked forward to being with them. My chaperone carried a folder; I carried my prison-issued items. She seemed slightly awkward, perhaps embarrassed, to have to explain, "The marshals put you down as suicidal, so we have to keep you on suicide watch."

"Suicide watch? I'm not suicidal."

With a pleasant, assertive tone that didn't let on she'd heard my statement, she continued, "Cuz it's Friday evening, you'll be here till Monday when the psychiatrist comes in. We keep an officer outside your door for observation 24/7. If you need toilet paper, ask her for it. You'll get four squares per use, and we need to watch you flush all four squares."

The escorting officer stopped short of the laughter further down the hall.

"Don't they need a reason to put me in here? I have never been suicidal. I didn't do anything to make them think I was suicidal. How can they just put that on my record with no reason?"

The officer persisted, "I need you to change into this paper gown and give me all your clothes." She held out a tissue-thin yellow gown. I could see her face through it perfectly.

"I can keep my underwear, bra, and socks, right?"

"No, I need everything. This paper gown will be the only clothing you wear."

"But I can see right through it." I looked around. "Where's the bed?"

"No bed. You'll sleep on the floor."

"Pillow?"

"Nope."

"Can I have a book?"

"No books, no paper, no pen. If you're good, we'll let you keep your glasses."

I removed my clothes and placed them in a laundry bag with my other items and donned the paper pajamas. With a mocking tone, I thought, *Like a good little girl.*

My eyebrows raised as if I'd spoken out loud. A sarcastic snarl twisted my lips as a couple of words barely slipped into audible, "Monday. This ought to be fun."

"Here's a blanket. You can use it to lay on or to cover up with."

The dark green, slightly padded blanket seemed better suited for a horse. The officer was right. It was oblong at about three feet by five feet and served only to separate me from the cold floor or to provide meager modesty but not both.

The floor drained my warmth like the room drained my spirit. The sterile fluorescent light stole my deeper sleeps, the cold paper gown raped my decency. Punishment. Pure and simple. Nobody had my best interest in mind in this place.

By dinner time, a new shift had transitioned my suicide sentry, "How do I eat?"

"With your fingers. No utensils—you might hurt yourself." This guard emoted a hardness, as if I inconvenienced her or worse, perhaps I turned her stomach.

"They're fucking plastic spoons! Who can hurt themselves with a plastic spoon?" Rage and helplessness boiled up inside and threatened to overtake my sanity. Animals received better treatment. The officer made a note in the log.

*I have no rights. No rights at all. I can't demand a spoon. I can't demand clothes. Hell! I can't even demand five squares of toilet paper. Oh God, how did I get here? I don't think I can make it through until Monday. I can't survive this. I can't. I've reached my limit. This is the end. It's too much, God! It's too much!*

The Catholic God of my childhood denied me his presence. I yearned for a faith I could feel. I needed a God that would hear me. I desperately needed a God that would understand what I was going through. I longed for the innocence and joy of a little girl in her favorite dress with orange and pink stripes, not the horror of this yellow tissue drape.

Time crawled.

*I'm still here, God. I'm still here. Looks like I am making it—no thanks to you! What have I done to make those marshals think I was suicidal? Do I want to kill myself? If I do, how would I do it? Is there a way that wouldn't hurt? Why doesn't my voice matter? I should know if I'm suicidal. I told them I wasn't. Can't they hear me? What time is it? There's no clock in this damn room.*

I could imagine Jessica's voices.

*Am I now hearing voices too? Am I crazy? Has this weekend made me crazy? This is unjust and unfair. Is unjust and unfair my new norm? I refuse to accept that! I will find a way to make it through this.*

One officer asked me why I was on suicide watch.

"I have no idea. I shouldn't be here. I think they're just trying to punish me. Maybe they put me in here because I'm a 'high profile' inmate."

"You're not the only big case in here. We have Lisa Montgomery."

She waited for my response. I shrugged. "Lisa Montgomery. Don't you know her? Cut a baby out of some pregnant woman."

I shook my head. I faintly remembered the headlines, but the name meant nothing to me. "Maybe you'll meet her. Be careful though." The officer gestured with a fist beside and above her head as though yanking an imaginary noose around her neck. She tipped her head and stuck out her tongue then continued, "Who could do such a thing?"

Saturday slid into Sunday. I could hear the women down the hall cheering for the Chiefs. I ached for a good Chiefs game. They never watched them at TCF. I listened carefully, trying to determine who was winning by the muffled shouts and tone of the cheers. I silently joined in.

I barely noticed my see-through gauzy gown anymore. I was cold. Another suicide sentry shift change. The officer who brought me here on Friday night returned. She pulled out a magazine. "I like to read out loud. Would that bother you? I can't help it if you just happen to overhear..."

*A blessing*, I thought as I listened to her read. *Another blessing on this journey. I can make it through whatever the system throws at me.*

When she finished reading, I decided to take a risk. "Have you looked at this room? It's filthy and I'm lying on the floor. Would it be possible for me to clean it?" She brought me a bucket and a mop. Like so many decades before, I avoided the pain of my circumstances while losing myself in work. I stretched my cell cleaning into hours.

*A mop and bucket are allowed, but a book and a pillow are not.*

First thing Monday morning, I sat in Dr. McCandless's office practically naked with my hands cuffed tightly behind my back, my arms clenched in an awkward effort to conceal myself with my blanket, which had precariously slipped down during my shuffling walk. After a weekend without sleep, what behavior would convince Dr. McCandless that I was normal, or at least sane, under such extreme conditions?

*At least Dr. McCandless is a woman.*

"Do you consider yourself suicidal?" she asked.

"Well, not until they put me on suicide watch! This whole experience is not fit for birds. Whoever dreamt up this treatment of suicidal inmates must have been crazy themselves!" I countered.

"Why do you think they noted in your file that you were suicidal?"

"Maybe they thought I should be. Maybe they thought I had to be crazy to break a convicted murderer out of prison and go on the run with him. Maybe they wanted me to be crazy so they could rest easy at night, not wondering if their wives might do something just as stupid and out of character. Maybe they were just plain mean and thought it should be part of my punishment. I guess if you really want to know, you'll have to ask them because I truly have no idea. I spent all of one hour with them. I don't see how they could know anything about me."

Whatever reassurance she was looking for that day must have come through because she freed me to join the Chiefs fans down the hall. A solitary black woman sat on one of the six bunks reading her Bible when I stumbled in.

"Here's your new roommate. She just came from suicide

watch."

My cellmate or "cellie" watched the officer leave, then slowly swept her gaze to me with her chin down and her eyes up, scrutinizing me. A lilting voice with a soft Jamaican accent said, "You gonna be okay? 'Cuz, we don't need no crazy up in heayah."

I nodded. I wasn't crazy. My freedom from suicide watch proved it.

I learned my new roommate's name was Faith, and as I'd heard in her accent she was in fact Jamaican. Faith became my first best friend in prison. She kept everyone calm with her belief in God and prayers for us all.

A short time later, I met my other roommates. Our room, designed to hold four inmates, held eight. An extra bunk bed had been squeezed inside the door and two women slept in boats— molded plastic trays which held mattresses. The boats were not elevated at all, and it was hard for older inmates to push out of them in the mornings. Nobody wanted to be in a boat.

The boats also made it difficult to move around in the cell. The eight of us shared one toilet, open to the whole room. We stored our extra set of clothes under our mattresses, which were just a bit shorter than our bed frames, creating a space at the end of our mattresses where I set up a little library of sorts. Overcrowded, most of us ate our meals sitting on our bunks.

Some of my roommates, like Faith, Betty, and Maria, made lasting impressions. Other names and faces drifted in and out as women left for prison or court appearances in other states. Nobody went home from CCA. You had to go to a federal prison facility to be released.

I shared a room with bank robbers, embezzlers, and drug mules. By far, most female federal inmates came by conspiracy charges, trumped-up federal charges that enabled the feds to give stiff sentences to the wives, mothers, and girlfriends of drug-dealing men. These women didn't necessarily actively participate, but conspiracy sentences had longer minimums than armed bank robbery.

Expensive and inefficient, the war on drugs pardoned the undercover federal agent sampling his crack purchase but imprisoned the crack dealer's wife for a decade. I never understood the logic.

With all the chaos and madness present in the overcrowded pod, I preferred to stay in my room with Faith, who sat on her bunk reading or writing to her two kids.

As a single parent of two young children back on the west coast, Faith had a lot on her mind, but never so much that she turned someone away who needed comfort as they navigated their own painful circumstances. Faith lifted us all. She showed us how to believe in ourselves.

J-Pod and K-Pod faced each other from across a common hallway and housed women at CCA. Wire-reinforced, tempered-glass windows lined the hallway. Officers from the central control room observed inmates and operated individual cell doors. Open showers skirted a single TV hung on the wall above the pod door. Women watching TV also watched showering women. Personal modesty violations further dehumanized inmates.

The sheer density of women showering within the two allotted hours developed a hotbed of arguments and fights. Tiny, paper-thin towels along the wall reserved an inmate's place in line for the showers, but since they all looked alike, arguments broke out.

The first and second users enjoyed clean showers, but slimy, little black worms appeared thereafter from the drains, wiggling and writhing underfoot. Worse still, black mold bloomed across our cell walls, inches from our faces while sleeping.

Once a month or so, officers would call everyone out into the dayroom and spray the walls of our cells with bleach to keep the mold at bay. It always came back, just like those little black worms.

However, CCA offered one joyous activity in the form of a crafting program. That's where I met my next two best friends, both named Lisa.

## 12

## EMILY'S SCENT

**A LIFESAVER, THE CRAFT PROGRAM** at CCA began as the vision of an elderly woman from the nearby community who volunteered to start a quilting class for the incarcerated women.

Between the two pods, a meeting room doubled as a library and church service room. Once a week Mrs. Smith would show up with bags full of fabric scraps from her own quilting projects and teach us how to piece together something beautiful; not enough fabric for a quilt, but we had fun inventing things to make for our families. I finished a table centerpiece for my mom, pillows for my sisters, and a couple of placemats for others.

There were no sewing machines and we stitched everything by hand. At the control center I exchanged my badge for a needle. Occasionally, when a needle dropped to the floor, we'd scramble to find it, since a lost needle meant no more crafts. We all loved this creative outlet so much that we preserved the privilege at all costs.

The officers began to see the value in the crafting program and would schedule crafts several times throughout the week, even without Mrs. Smith. Each of us were given a plastic trash bag with our name on it to store our projects. The bags were collected by an officer at the end of a crafting period and locked away in the control room.

In my first class, overwhelmed by the possibilities, I fumbled through the pile of fabric scraps dumped on the table. Most pieces were tiny slivers of fabric, insignificant to anyone from the real world, but in prison, none of them were considered too small to be of use. Part of the joy was figuring out how to make something from nothing.

Repurposing fabric scraps made me feel a kinship with my grandmother. The twelfth of thirteen children born deep in the Ozarks, Grandma grew up making quilts to keep her family warm. Her quilts were not the fancy coordinated designer fabric projects that most women make now; I'm talking about real quilts, a hodgepodge of any fabric on hand from worn shirts, linings of old flannel coats and stained aprons.

I found myself sitting at the same table with two other women I hadn't met. They were housed in J-Pod, across the hall. They introduced themselves as "The Lisas."

To keep things less confusing, the shorter Lisa volunteered, "My nickname as a kid was George, so just call me George, and it will be less confusing. I like being called George anyway."

I learned to call her George, but I thought of them as My Two Lisas.

George came to CCA around the same time I did, and Lisa had been there much longer. Picked up on a conspiracy charge, George had spent years begging her husband to stop selling drugs and nearly achieved her goal, but the feds deemed her guilty because she neglected to turn him in.

The other Lisa turned out to be the infamous Lisa Montgomery, mentioned by my guard during suicide watch.

I studied Lisa carefully. I saw nothing frightening. Both indicted, Lisa and I showed up on the evening news on a regular basis and that drew me to her. We were members of the high-profile-criminals-that-the-media-loves-to-sensationalize club.

The two Lisas bunked together in J-Pod. But both pods shared activities, church, outdoor rec, and crafts, so I got to spend quite a bit of time with My Two Lisas. The biggest reason I went to everything that was offered, was to be able to spend time with my new friends.

The Lisas were crafting queens. Our crafting sessions soon included tatting as well. Tatting is an old-fashioned way of making lace, using fingers to create loops through which a shuttle passed. Tatters use shuttles to hold their silk thread. We made do with sewing thread wrapped around a piece of cardboard.

Both Lisas tatted the most beautiful, complicated things. I on the other hand, struggled and lacked the patience to be good at doing things slowly. The loops would slip off my fingers and my dangling thread would twist into a complicated knot. Lisa would always salvage my mess.

I explained to Mom that Lisa rescued most of the tatting projects I made. She didn't listen though and bragged to all her friends, showing off the beautiful, tatted masterpieces that I gave her.

Lisa and I laughed about it often. When I'd bring her some pathetic mess, she'd say, "Let's see what I'm making your mom today."

The glass and phones of CCA that separated me from Mom disappointed me most; no more hugs, games, or shared food between us.

Mom met the Lisas in the visiting room and liked them both. She didn't have a chance to meet Faith since Faith's family lived too far away to visit.

Allowed two visitors at a time for one hour on Friday evenings, occasionally, a sister would accompany Mom, but often, she came alone.

Mom never considered Lisa's crime and she didn't even ask about George's. She always greeted them warmly and talked to their families when they were all waiting in an outer room to be admitted before visiting hour started.

My sisters on the other hand, asked me to point out Lisa as if she were some macabre celebrity. "Is she here? Do you know her? Which one is she? Are you scared? What's she like?"

Lisa was just Lisa, my friend. I could see the person beyond her crime and was willing to give her a chance.

One day Lisa went to court leaving George and me crafting without her. Sometimes, George knew what others needed but given the nature of Lisa's crime, neither of us felt comfortable discussing babies, births, or pregnancies. Lisa's absence gave George the greenlight we'd been waiting for; we could discuss our children without making Lisa feel awkward.

George started the conversation. "I have three older children and then Burt and I had Sabrina. But Sabrina had a twin who died at birth." I stopped tatting; my body flushed with feeling. George continued, "She's my youngest and she's struggling without me. She's only six. She needs her mom."

I looked down at the tatting shuttle in my hands, "My children are grown; I have two boys. Eric, the oldest, graduates from college in May. We're close and run a web design business together. Well, we did. Greg is four years younger and hasn't decided what to do. Between them, I had a daughter who only lived eighteen hours and thirty-one minutes. My husband forbade us from talking about her because it only made me cry."

"Oh Toby. I'm so sorry." George sat staring with a furrowed brow and her eyes welling.

Nobody spoke for a long moment until I continued. "In the last couple of months of my pregnancy, I sensed a difference in my baby. I couldn't quite put my finger on it, but she didn't move much, and I wasn't very big. I kept having nightmares about how many pallbearers you need for a baby. But nobody listened to me. My doctor told me, 'Second-time mothers always sense problems when there aren't any.' My mom kept telling me my baby would be fine, but Mom was mistaken."

George listened and contemplated. Then she said, "Mothers do have a sixth sense about their babies."

"When I was in labor, I kept my face to the wall and closed my eyes to what my heart already knew, somehow sensing that the only chance this baby had was to stay inside me. Her name was Emily Anne Elizabeth, and she was born holding life in one hand and heaven in the other."

George spoke up, "That's a beautiful name."

I nodded, appreciating her compliment, then continued, "I held my breath, waiting to hear something, anything from my baby. 'Breathe baby breathe,' I willed. The silence was broken, but not by her. A NICU team rushed into the room, and everything shifted to high speed. Then they took her away.

"They took me to a room across from the nursery, the cries of newborn babies triggered changes in my body. My breasts filled with milk that my daughter could not drink. I was helpless to stop the flow and the breast milk soaked my gown. My husband turned from my trouble and within minutes left for home. I waited all night for somebody to tell me something. Anything. But nobody came."

"Nobody gave you any news at all. The entire night?"

"Nope, but the next day I learned it was because my husband told them to let me sleep and not to let me see our baby. In the morning a nurse stopped in, and she told me the NICU was at the end of the hall and of course I could see my baby. As I walked down that long hall, I could see joyous mothers and babies in every room I passed. And I hated them all."

George handed me a tissue.

"She had so many problems; blind and deaf, hydrocephalus, microcephaly, a diaphragmatic hernia, spina bifida, and the thing that freaked Rob out and caused him to request I not see her—a double cleft palate…"

I felt George squeezing my hand.

"My mom and a family friend, Father Davern, came. We took turns holding her while Father Davern baptized her. I remember he said, 'Emily was blessed to have been born in the night and lived to see the light of day. She felt her mother's love. What more could we ask?'

"I wanted to scream out, 'Time! I'd ask for more time. This isn't enough. I want clocks to stop.' But you can't stop time or turn back clocks. After she died, the hospital staff unhooked, unplugged, and dressed her tiny body and took us to a private room. We had an hour to be with her, love her, and hold her. I clipped a whisp of her soft, red hair, buried my face in her neck and inhaled deeply, drinking in the scent of my daughter, trying to gather enough to last a lifetime."

Tears streamed down my face as George wrapped me in a hug. Twenty-five years hadn't been long enough to recover from Emily's death. My tears didn't represent *some* sad memories. My tears carried a quarter of a century of unexpressed grief.

I continued my story, "My dad was at work. Back then we didn't have cell phones, of course, so nobody called him to tell him about Emily. And after everyone went home that evening, Dad walked into my room carrying this tiny little sachet that he'd bought in the gift shop. My dad doesn't buy gifts, so this was extra special. When I saw him walk in, my heart broke because I realized he didn't know."

I paused, remembering, "He said, 'tell me about your baby, Toby.' And I had to say, to the person I'd spent my whole life trying to impress, my baby was dead. Once those words came out of my mouth, it made everything so real."

"What did your dad say, Toby?"

"I could see the struggle in his face. And then he whispered, 'We have an angel in the family.' Dad sat with me in silence for nearly an hour, holding my hand, then he told me, 'We'll get through this, Toby. We'll get through it.' And he left. I wanted to run after him and be anywhere but in that hospital room.

The weight of the moment settled on me, "It's been more than twenty years, and this is the most I've ever talked about her. Burying my grief was the worst thing that I could have done. I didn't have anyone to guide me through this pain. I had no idea where to start. George, you're the first person I've met who has also lost a baby." I shook my head. "I should have talked about Emily. I needed to embrace my loss; not push it away. It should have never been the secret I carried around for decades, afraid to make others uncomfortable.

"My secret poisoned me. I became a master of deceit. I buried myself in sacrifice to the lives and needs of the people around me. If sadness emerged from the depths of my grief, I'd stack another project onto the cross of my own crucifixion walk. No exhaustion, no penance, no kindness, no contemplation, and no denial kept the loss of her from shredding my soul. If I let my guard down, surely, I would never find myself again."

George's wisdom sometimes reflected obvious painful realities. "Well, we can talk about all the hard things in here. In fact, I think we must."

I took in George's words. She was right. If difficult things couldn't be covered in a difficult place, then where could they be? "After Emily died, I smothered Eric, hovering over him, protecting him from heartache, from falling out of trees, from slipping on the ice, from the freedom of living a childhood wild with discovery and curiosity. Oh, but my dad, my dad watched carefully, waiting for me to see the truth myself. When he realized it was beyond me, he told me, 'Toby, let the boy be a boy. He wants to climb a tree. Let him go. I know you're scared and want to protect him, but God won't do that to you again.' I don't think I ever truly let Eric be free, though.

George simply waited while I told my story. "And then I decided maybe another baby would fill this black hole in my life. So I became pregnant with our third child. I hoped for a girl to fill Emily's empty room. We all 'knew' this third baby was a girl. The doctors even suggested so.

I chuckled slightly through the tears I shared with George at the memory of what happened next, "When they took me back to my room, my parents were waiting. They asked, 'Is she healthy, Toby? Ten toes, ten fingers?' I told them, 'Yes! Ten fingers, ten toes and one more appendage I didn't expect; it's a boy!'

George laughed for a moment, until she felt my chill.

"George, I blinded myself to the truth. An overt, outright lie would have done less damage. I simply could not see that I expected Emily to be my conduit to enjoy a little girl's dearly missed childhood. I expected Emily to somehow, miraculously, draw my family back to a loving center. Oblivious to Rob's plight, I couldn't get out of my own way enough to see a different path back to my marriage. I resented Rob. Life had been unkind and unfair. I resented God. I resented pregnant women, little girls, and the color pink. I feigned happiness while I buried grief.

George stared back at me, I continued, "I think the end of my marriage came before Emily's death, but Rob coped his way, and I coped mine. Together we killed what little remained. For the next twenty-three years, we pretended.

"After Rob and I killed the marriage, I killed myself to be there for baseball practices, 4-H shows, mealtimes, and so much more. Heck, I even shored up dwindling self-esteems and defended the boys from their father. However, even with all that, the boys deserved better.

"By the time the boys left home, two decades of hard labor and projects gave way and left me standing in my living room wondering 'Who's that guy in the recliner?' I don't know that I ever loved Rob, but I did know that I didn't hate him." I took a deep breath. She searched my eyes for answers. "It was worse than that, George. Apathy, a complete absence of feeling, pushed me into John's arms."

In this most unlikely of places, rusty old chains fell away under the sweet confinement of prison bars, and I finally began to heal.

# 13.

## POD CAST

"**CRAFTS IN TEN MINUTES!** Crafts, ten minutes!"

From a dead sleep, I exploded out of my bunk and scurried over and under and through other sleeping women. I dressed quickly; latecomers weren't allowed. With a bit of a leap across our polished concrete floor, I cleared the two sleeping women in their boats to a heap of nylon laundry bags inside the door. Landing on the bags, one foot slid one way and my other foot crumpled beneath me, trying to stop the slide. The sound of my fall echoed through the pod.

Opening the door, an officer appeared. "Young, are you alright?"

"Sure! I'm just getting ready for crafts." I stood up but my leg wouldn't hold me, and I crumpled to the floor again, this time in a significant amount of physical pain that overtook the embarrassment of the fall.

"I'm okay," I groaned and crawled to the dayroom where I pulled myself up onto a stool.

"You're going to medical."

"No! Please don't send me there. Let me go to crafts. If it still hurts after crafts, I'll go to medical."

The radio crackled, "Young in K-Pod needs an escort to

medical."

I sighed. Medical visits took the entire day. Uncomfortable, crowded, and eternally mundane, medical allowed no books or magazines. An inmate could wait for hours, and through several counts, before being seen. They'd say you were going to see a doctor, but no doctors actually worked there. A visiting doctor showed up once every couple of weeks to review the cases diagnosed by the doctors, who weren't really doctors. Medical was the last place anyone wanted to go.

An officer arrived to escort me, but when I stood up, I fell again, writhing in pain. "We need a wheelchair in K-Pod."

I sat in medical holding on a hard plastic chair through two head counts before being seen. My leg throbbed more with each passing minute. "Ms. Young? This way please."

Looking over the top of his glasses, without even touching my leg, today's "wannabe-doctor" made an immediate diagnosis. "Fell, huh? Well, you've probably sprained your ankle. I'll give you a pair of crutches. Let's see… today is Wednesday; you can use the crutches until Saturday. If it's still bothering you on Monday, you can order some aspirin on commissary if you have funds in your account."

After five hours, I hobbled back to the pod. "Sprained ankle," I called out to the crowd of women gathering around me.

"Oh, don't feel bad, they canceled crafts this morning anyway. You didn't miss a thing." Betty volunteered, "I'm giving you my bottom bunk. I'll take your top one. That was quite a fall this morning. The laundry bags are gone, we decided to keep them in the corner out of the way from now on. That was dumb to put them in front of the door."

Bottom bunks were precious and scarce; nobody ever offered one freely. I felt loved and cared for. Later that afternoon, lying in my new bottom bunk, I watched as new colors bruised across my left leg, and I caught a bit of conversation.

"Thank goodness you found that needle, Betty! We'd still be in there if you hadn't."

I sat up. "Wait a minute. You said crafts were canceled."

"Oh." Everyone looked sheepish. "It wasn't really canceled, we just wanted to make you feel better. We know how much you love crafts."

Instead of lamenting my loss of a precious crafts session this close to Christmas, I basked in the love of these women who had become family. My sisters, who were blood family, banished me to the choir loft, yet these women who had nothing more to give than a bottom bunk and a story, loved me and gave all. Unconditionally. Pure love and concern for someone else meant everything.

By evening, my leg was grotesquely swollen.

"Look at all those colors!"

"Green, black, purple, red."

"That doesn't look like a sprain to me."

"Can you move your toes?"

I could, with a lot of pain. Faith laid her hands on my ankle and prayed. Betty rubbed lotion. Maria handed me a tamale. My roommates, like a flock of mother hens, cackled over me, offering to get my dinner tray, read me a story, and anything else they could think of to ease my pain.

On Saturday, as instructed, I tried to stand without my crutches but crumpled to the floor. By Sunday morning, my leg looked grim.

Ms. Johnston, one of the few more pleasant guards, began her shift at midnight. My posse ambushed Ms. Johnston to my side, demanding action.

"Look at her leg!" seven pleading voices chimed in at once on my behalf.

"Something needs to happen."

"It's getting worse."

"She moans all night long."

Ms. Johnston winced at the sight of my leg, "What have they done for you?"

I answered, "Nothing. Gave me crutches. Denied me a pillow to prop my leg on."

"Pain meds?"

"Nope, they said I could order aspirin on commissary."

"I'll be back as soon as count is over."

An hour later, Ms. Johnston marched in with a pillow. "It's the least I can do. Prop your leg up on that. I'll be back shortly."

After a trip to medical, she had even better news. "The real doctor will be in tomorrow. I put you on his list. He'll see you first thing in the morning."

The next morning, back in medical, Dr. Wannabe stood by uncomfortably as the real doctor examined my leg.

"This is no sprain. What did the x-ray show?"

Although his question wasn't directed to me, I answered. "I never had an x-ray or any pain meds. I was told to order aspirin on today's commissary, but I won't get that until Thursday."

Dr. Wannabe furtively looked around the room, wishing himself somewhere else.

On Thursday a portable machine arrived. I finally got an x-ray.

Friday morning a call came over the speaker, "Young, get ready to go out."

"Where am I going?"

"To get a cast put on your broken leg."

It turned out even wheelchair-bound inmates with broken legs must be shackled during transport. As if I could go anywhere. No cuff would fit around my broken ankle, so they used three zip ties threaded together.

Ashamed to be out in public in a bright orange outfit with INMATE emblazoned across my back, I kept my eyes lowered.

The orthopedic doctor's office occupied space in the heart of downtown, across the street from the antique mall that Mom and I loved to visit. Oh, how I longed for shopping with Mom.

Homesickness threatened to overturn my composure.

With my hands and feet shackled, and an armed corrections officer on either side of me, the message to the other patients in the waiting room inferred *high-risk, dangerous criminal, beware!*

As their freak show, I felt strengthened; I straightened up and boldly stared back, past my shame. I stared at them from behind the orange jumpsuit. I stared at them from between the guards and across the magazines—those magazines with smiling, entitled, do-gooder celebrities that mocked the rest of a jealous world while they rested atop the coffee table between us. I stared fearlessly. I stared, and with my eyes, without a word, I announced to those people that I refuse. My laser eyes said, *Think what you like, I am not scum! I am Toby, yet to be defined!*

The doctor held my new set of x-rays to the light. "This is bad. It's a considerable break. Broken in two places, misaligned. It must be reset. How long ago did this happen?"

"Ten days," I answered.

The doctor looked to the officer for confirmation. He then dropped his hands to his sides, "That's too long to reset in the office. We'll need to take her to surgery, rebreak it, and set it properly."

The officer responded immediately as if this question had been anticipated, "We can't authorize surgery. What other options do we have?"

"Well, I can just put a cast on it and hope it finds its way back together properly. She'll probably have trouble with it in the future. It's not the best option. She should have been here ten days ago."

The officer answered for us, "We'll take the second option."

The doctor sighed, "Okay, I'll cast it up, no promises."

Looking at me, he added, "What color would you like?"
*Color! I can pick a color!*

"Bright pink."

The cast relieved some of the pain. After six weeks, the hot pink cast would be replaced with a purple one and then an orange one, until finally the bones had mended enough to wear a boot and hobble around with one crutch. My healing process would take more than five months because of poor care and a simple delay in taking an x-ray in a reasonable amount of time, leading to a misdiagnosis.

Outraged at my treatment—or, more specifically, *lack thereof*—my public defender pushed me to sue CCA and the federal government after being released from prison. Inmates don't have the right to legal action, but my release would come before the statute of limitations expired. As a public defender, my attorney couldn't represent me in a civil case, so he looked for another. However, like most felons without resources, I attracted no one willing to take on CCA and the U.S. Marshals. I felt violated by a system that dehumanized all inmates. Minus other choices, I moved on without looking back.

# 14.

## RUSTING ARMOR

AFTER OUR CAPTURE, AFTER OUR separation, John persisted. He wrote messages to the media and had them published in the paper for me to read. He smuggled letters to me while we did time. He even passed verbal messages through inmates.

I have no idea how he knew my whereabouts or with whom I shared space, but he mastered the dark art of forbidden prison communication. Sometimes other inmates hand delivered notes and messages to me. Sometimes I'd find them laying on my bunk.

One letter proclaimed, "I'm your knight in shining armor." I almost expected John to one day bust through the concrete blocks to save me. My heart melted every time I pictured him riding to my rescue. Doggedly, he pursued me.

Each time I'd think I was over him; another song, poem, or drawing would erode my resolve. Still so in love with him, I filled long spaces of empty time yearning for him, imagining him, dreaming about what we could have done better, worrying about him, and obsessing over every inch of him.

*Had I ruined his life by helping him escape?*

Where was he? Was he okay?

I copied one of his letters into my journal.

*December 14, 2006*

*I can't get you out of my mind. I keep thinking about how much I enjoyed talking with you, how great you looked when you smiled, and how much I like your laugh. I daydream about you off and on all day, replaying pieces of our conversation... laughing again about funny things you said or did. I've memorized your face and the way you look at me... it melts my heart every time I think about it. And I catch myself smiling when I imagine what will happen the next time we're together. You must be something really special because I can't remember the last time I felt so strongly about someone. Even though neither of us knows what the future holds, I know one thing for sure... you're one of the very best things that's happened to me in a long time. It's been a year now; I still love you as I did a year ago. I have no regrets. Always thinking of you. Love ya, Baby.*

"Girl, he love you!" my cellmates reassured me. They were in awe of his determination to rescue me. Except for Faith. She firmly believed I needed to let him go.

"You won't leave him as long as you think of him. If you help him in any way, you're still there with him, even though you're not 'with' him. You can't risk your freedom anymore. You've done enough. Let him go," she implored.

That was a hard thing to even fathom for me. He was my wildest romantic dreams come true in a lot of ways.

I wrote in my journal:

*Let go of him, then memories come. I can't let go. I try and try and try. What is the hold? Everyone says to let go—no future there. I know they're right. But then I close my eyes and dream and I remember everything. I worry about him and wonder what he's doing. I hope for him, and I pray for him. I let it go on the surface, but deep down, I want to be with him again. I remember every word, every movement. I remember even the times when he was mad, and I was scared. And still I can't let go. At least not completely. I'm making progress, I guess that's all I can do. Baby steps—eventually I'll get there but I don't go willingly. If I turn away, what will he have? No one. Nothing at all. What kind of person can do that to someone? But I need a life too. I want to have someone in my life more than just through letters. Is that too much to ask? Is it too much to hope for? And, maybe no one will want me anyway...*

Written by Toby while at CCA Federal Prison, December 2006

Gradually, I began to realize that true love—healthy love—would never ask someone to put themselves in danger. But on the flip side, true love is sacrificial. True love would do anything for another person regardless of consequence.

For John, I sacrificed my safety, freedom, and integrity. I paid heavy consequences for a spin around the world with John Manard. And John paid a significant price for our escape as well.

Through my own depravity, I wasn't thinking clearly. My mind, suspended in the euphoria of our romance, left me with no capacity to count the cost for myself, or for John, or my family. I never believed our plan would fail, yet, at the same time, I never thought we'd really do it. I was moving through life in an altered state with emotions weary from decision fatigue, multi-tasking, and in a steady state of distraction, being pulled too thin on every front. Lack of emotional input and support paralyzed me to life's demand of duty and had done nothing to refill all the tanks that ran dry since I was a five-year-old girl stepping into significant responsibility.

People wanted to call me a victim, but I refused. Sensing that, far from relieving me of responsibility, it would lock me in an even more dastardly trap named *victimhood*. It would take me more than a year, but I started to let go of the idea of John and me.

Heartbroken, I loved him. No one would understand. And no one could sympathize with my shattered heart. I would face this mountain alone for the rest of my life. Society dictated that it was not okay to love a person with a conviction of murder over their head, whether they were guilty or not.

But the views of society aren't what drove my decision to move on. I knew I couldn't find myself and stand on my own while leaning on someone else for my self-worth. To heal, I had to see the world through my own eyes. I had to discover just who Toby really was.

## 15

# GRACE, LOST AND FOUND

**ALL EIGHT OF US IN CELL 106** faced Christmas 2006 as our first behind bars. With a new, bright pink cast on my leg and a yearning heart, sleep hid from me. One not-so-starry night when we all tossed and turned, I saw Faith lying awake. Dim lights splashed over into our room like sunshine on an overcast day, emitted from the fluorescents above the dayroom.

I asked, "Tell us what your family has for Christmas dinner."

"Ooooh, in Jamaica we eat gooood! Rum pudding, jerked chicken, curry goat, garnished hens, and oxtail with beans."

"Sounds interesting. I don't know about the oxtail though," I said.

Maria propped up on one elbow with her face in her hand.

"How about you, Maria?"

"TAMALES! With pork, cheese, and jalapeños. We'll also steam sweet tamales with raisins, coconut, pineapple, peanuts, sugar, masa, and baking powder."

Pam spoke up next, "We ain't gotta special menu for Christmas, but I'll tell you, I miss garage sales with my mom. We be drivin' real slow and always stoppin' at the stupid ones."

Each of us shared family traditions and drifted away from prison, if only for a moment.

Maria spoke up, "Betty and I will cook you a Mexican Christmas dinner this year!"

The Mexican women brought a talent for whipping up a feast made from the junk on commissary and bits of food from our meal trays. Somehow, they made delicious tamales with bags of Fritos and milk, filling them with meat scavenged from dinner. We all gathered round when Maria and Betty planned a meal, contributing whatever ingredients we could.

Creative ideas flew as women offered ways to celebrate behind bars.

"I know!" Maria urgently whispered, "I'll do colored pencil drawings on envelopes for each one of us and we'll hang them on the lockers." Maria, a talented and gifted artist, earned extra commissary by drawing for other inmates.

Faith chimed in, "Let's each of us put something in the envelopes as gifts."

Betty added, "Yeah, it could be something from commissary or something we make."

Pam piped up, "It could be a favor we promise to someone, like takin' their turn at cleaning."

I bought candy bars and popcorn for each cellmate, and I wrote a poem for the whole room. Maria copied it onto a custom-colored piece of paper that she decorated, and we hung it in our window. The other women in the pod complimented the décor and wanted to join. Energy bustled as each cell found ways to decorate for the holiday. And then, someone had a brilliant idea.

"Let's have a Christmas talent show!"

Women scurried around with smiles on their faces as they prepared their talent show entries. The pod bubbled with joy. Perhaps prison provided the context. Perhaps Christmas didn't require department stores and light displays. The Christmas star shone brightest in the shadows of our circumstances.

Shortly after midnight on Christmas Eve, a woman started

singing "Silent Night" into the quiet and darkened pod. Others joined in the hauntingly beautiful serenade while tears streamed from the most hardened faces. I imagined apparitions of despair waltzing with ghosts of joy. I missed my mom and my dad and my boys.

The next day, jeers, laughs, and applauses erupted while talent show events entertained us. Singers sang, actors performed skits, and storytellers regaled us. The infection truly revealed its contagion when officers, who had been standing at the rear of the pod, one with hands on her belt and the other with arms crossed in front of her, joined us while singing Christmas carols. After all, who could resist a little "Rudolph, the Red-Nosed Reindeer" at Christmas time? Through it all, no one felt their broken hearts, we felt like family.

Christmas the way I imagined it might have been on the cold isolated prairie a hundred years before. People with little more than a pot to piss in reaching out to other pot-less people. I believe the true Christmas spirit lived more vibrantly behind bars than anywhere else in my life. We celebrated Christmas and it was good. Beyond good, it was special and memorable.

And blessed.

I got mail every day and it kept my spirits up. But one day, I got a letter from a sister that forced me to take a long look at myself and at her.

The first sentence of her lengthy letter let me know that she "...could forgive me for what I'd done but she could never forgive me for killing Dad, because if he wasn't worried about me, his chemo would have worked."

I found her letter a bit toxic, but I responded:

*Sister,*

*I'm sure that it feels good to get all of that off your chest. It seems like it was an awfully heavy load. I hope writing that helps you heal and move forward.*

*I have never said to anyone that 'I couldn't help what I did.' What I said is that I couldn't explain why I made the choice I did. I've thought about it a lot and am getting closer to understanding it— which is why my therapist advised me to quit trying to explain the past and put my energy into healing, moving forward, and re-building my life.*

*That does not mean I have NOT accepted responsibility or that I am not remorseful. I have apologized to Rob and the boys, to Mom and Dad, and to all of you. What exactly are you looking for in my remorsefulness?*

*My sitting with the family did not detract from Dad or his funeral. I do understand and accept that you felt Rob had more right to be at Dad's funeral than I did. Everyone is entitled to their own opinion. But the facts are I AM Dad's daughter. Period. You can't change that. I will never let you try to give me the responsibility for Dad's death. Dad would never condone anyone placing the blame for his death on any member of his beloved family and you know that.*

*I am not lonely in my prison cell. I did not have to suffer through Christmas alone. I had the best Christmas I may have ever experienced. I have roommates who hold me up and love me when I'm feeling down. Women who love me unconditionally. I am not sorry I'm here—strange as it may sound—because being here is creating the strong, wise, spiritual woman I was meant to be.*

*Being in prison is a place, it is not who I am.*

*Some people want answers I can't give. Not because I don't want to, but because I can't. I don't have those answers. I don't even have some of them.*

*I know this has affected the whole family and I am so, so sorry that my actions hurt you all. It has never been my nature to hurt. Even though it seems ridiculous now, I never thought anyone would even miss me. I know that I had an emotional breakdown. And why? For probably a million different little reasons that seemed insignificant individually, but together stacked up into an insurmountable mountain. The craziest thing is, at that moment in time, it seemed a good choice. And that's the saddest part of all.*

*I know that Rob has been around as long as you can remember. I know he carried you to bed when you were little. But, for every time he carried you to bed, Sister, I carried you 25 times. I want you to be friends with Rob. I'm not asking you to choose. I'm glad you've grown closer.*

*Verbal abuse is not having a temper. Verbal abuse is subtle continuous putdowns. Verbal abuse is almost always invisible to everyone outside of the relationship. Verbal abusers act one way in public and an entirely different way at home. Verbal abusers always sound like "such a nice guy." Verbal abuse and physical abuse are as different as night and day. The signs that you talked about identify someone who has been physically abused. I did not just wake up one day and say, "Oh, I think I was verbally abused." I, like you, didn't even know it was a thing.*

*I am not trying to blame him; I was only trying to tell MY family what MY life was like. If I had talked to someone at the time, my actions could have been so different. One of the most critical things I've learned is to talk the truth to someone. My biggest problem was holding everything in. I'm not making that mistake again. I made a terribly wrong choice for a mish mash of reasons.*

*Eleven months later, removed from all the emotions, my thoughts are becoming clearer. If I could go back in time and do things differently, I would. That's not an option. The best I can do is learn from my mistakes and not repeat them.*

*I know my boys are hurt and I write to them, pray for them, and try to call them. Anyone who counsels them that I have abandoned them and don't love them and that I am selfish and that I never had the intention of seeing them again is NOT doing so out of love for the boys. How can anything so hateful and hurtful make them feel better about themselves?*

Written by Toby while at CCA Federal Prison, January 2007

Before the escape, my sisters were my girlfriends. Without them, prison friends became sisters. As I got further into my healing journey, I decided many things for myself with the help of my newfound family.

I will not beg for love. I will not spend my entire life apologizing. I will move on. And I will move forward. I will never again let anyone try to tell me I am unworthy or less than. If this means that some people choose to remove themselves from my life, it's their choice—not mine. I must hold my head up and love myself. I will be my own champion.

I. Am. Worthy.

# 16.

## BURNED

OUR ROOMS REMAINED COLD year-round, but in the frigid months of winter, a thick coating of ice formed inside our windows like mini glaciers. I shivered beneath a cheap, ineffective, recycled plastic-bottles blanket. Prison food, with its inadequate rations of empty-calorie tastelessness, did nothing to stimulate my body to a warmer state of being. I retired nightly wearing long johns, sweatshirts, and a hat. Prison administrations, refined over thousands of years, knew best how to quietly impose discomforting conditions.

Faith collected empty soda bottles, filled them with water, microwaved them, and took them to bed to keep warm. Betty, ever the faithful servant, microwaved the bottles for Faith most evenings, until one night when all hell broke loose. Loud pops followed by shrieks came from the dayroom. Officers ran into the pod as Betty ran into our cell. Blabbering incoherent Spanish, Betty cried and grabbed at her shirt. As it happened, Betty opened the microwave door at the same instant that the bottles, weakened by the heat, exploded with scalding water.

We scrambled from our bunks and peeled Betty's clothes off. Her breasts burned bright red with heat radiating from them that we felt from six inches away. Officers looked at her injuries, decided she'd be okay, locked us in, and continued with evening count.

Betty cried all night. I couldn't sleep. Memories of the sights and sounds echoed in my mind from that May morning some forty-three years before. Betty cried and I buried my head in my pillow to muffle the sound as my mind replayed the nightmare...

*The budding leaves of the weeping willow tree unfurled and decorated their branches with hues of spring. Flocks of songbirds gathered in our backyard to chirp and chatter while I danced to their tunes. Daddy pulled at his leather gloves, one finger at a time, as I wrapped willow whips around my waist.*

*"Daddy, look, I'm a princess!"*

*"Yes, you are, Toby."*

*Lively willow branches cascaded over me into long leafy hair, and just as quickly, I reimagined them as a curtain to peek around, a view from my castle window.*

*Daddy continued pruning, cutting, and gathering my lovely branches.*

*I stomped my foot in protest, "Daddy, why do you want to cut them off? Now, I can't reach them to be a princess."*

*"They'll grow back, Toby, I just need them to be shorter so I can mow the grass under here."*

*"I can help, Daddy, watch me." I pulled some clippings to the pile Daddy had started near the burn barrel.*

*"Toby," Mom called from the kitchen window, "time to come in and get ready for school. Your bus will be here shortly."*

*Already, I loved kindergarten almost as much as helping Daddy. Through the basement door, past Daddy's ping pong table, and up the stairs, I undistractedly dashed by the faithful clock on the kitchen wall.*

*Tick.*

*Tick.*

*Tick.*

*My blonde hair, cut in a pixie, made it easier for Mom. I liked short hair. I liked that it was fluffy. I pulled my favorite dress over my head, the one with four decorative buttons under my chin. Encircled by pink and orange stripes, my very favorite colors. This dress made me happy.*

*The idyllic setting for a boisterous Catholic family, our house bustled with five children born in five years. Like so many afternoon routines, dishes clinked, drawers slid, and knives dipped into the mustard and mayonnaise jars as Mom made lunch amid my younger siblings.*

*Watching eagerly for my big yellow bus to arrive, the sound of a slogging step jostled me. Heavy. Deliberate. Foreboding. Unlike Daddy's normal sprint up the basement stairs. The clock ticked once then I heard the second step.*

*Tick.*

*Step.*

*Tick.*

*Step.*

*What could only be described as fear boiled up in me as Mom returned my glance.*

*"Daddy?" A bent and frail man shuffled into the hall. Acrid smells and foreign sounds flooded the space around us. "Daddy? Is that you?"*

*Daddy's glow withered beneath a menacing spirit which threatened us all. A strangely disturbed pain replaced his natural joy. His eyes fluttered as if trying to see something that wasn't there, perhaps a way out of this present horror or a way to turn back time.*

*Daddy focused on something beyond me. He didn't see me. I stood right there before him, but he couldn't see me.*

*Somehow, Daddy's spirit violently evicted from his broken body, waged war against a charred figure called Death. Before the gates of heaven, wielding a gleaming shield, Daddy thwarted every powerful blow. Each labored whisp of breath, for which he fought, divided by ticks of time, further isolated Daddy's spirit. The reflection in Daddy's eyes gave me a sense that the battle for his life included me.*

*The kitchen clock, now in the distance, advanced. Increments of time sprawled and echoed between Daddy's battle and our home, sounding more like a great clap of thunder than a tick.*

*Tick.*

*Tick.*

*Tick.*

*Eternities elapsed within me while a mere ten seconds delivered pieces of Daddy's spirit back to us. The stench of burned human flesh and hair filled the room. Daddy had no eyebrows or lashes. His ears looked like pieces of shriveled pumpkin. Smoldering crinkles zigzagged across his raw head. Bits of dirt embedded Daddy's bloody and oozing skin, a patchwork of mottled colors. His lips were swollen and distorted, like my Gumby doll. Scraps of smoldering cloth flaked to the floor, trailing little wisps of smoke behind. He held his arms out from his sides as though sitting in a big, invisible lounge chair. The black parts of his skin rolled down like melted wax and pooled like Mom's pantyhose when she took them off at night.*

*Horror hijacked my voice, my ability to communicate and my instinctual need to scream, paralyzing me where I stood. My legs turned to stone. Silent tears spilled to my cheeks. Mom stepped closer, my baby sister on her hip. The shock on her face etched this moment in my mind and confirmed the gut-wrenching fear in the pit of my tummy.*

*Mom's eyes met mine and, for a moment, I thought she might come to me and make everything okay.*

*I waited. I waited for her to promise me, the same way she reassured me when I crashed my bike into the sand at the bottom of the hill and shredded my knee. I waited for her to tell me this was nothing to cry about. I knew Mom was processing circumstances, and I held my breath waiting for Mom's answer to a question that had never been asked. I waited. The clock continued to tick.*

*Tick.*

*Tick.*

*Tick.*

*Daddy's eyes welled with tears while he struggled to remain calm.*

*When he finally found a voice, a quivering whisper desperately pleaded, "I need help."*

*Mom glanced back at me, and I intuitively took my baby sister.*

*Almost as if with divine intervention, Mom stepped away, out of life as we knew it and into Daddy's new world. With a mixed expression of love and fear, she gratuitously and gently patted Daddy's smoldering head with the tea towel from her shoulder until she realized the futility. As he started shaking uncontrollably, Mom pushed past him and grabbed a clean quilt from the morning's laundry, draping it lightly over his shoulders.*

*Stopping in front of him, Mom looked directly into Daddy's eyes, "Jim, it's me, Peg. We're going to get through this." With a barely perceptible nod he relinquished all control.*

*I stood watching with my baby sister's arms squeezed around my neck.*

*Picking up the telephone, Mom listened for a dial tone. I'd never seen her face more focused as her tender fingers pulled the rotary dial.*

*"Too far away for an ambulance. We'll have to drive ourselves."*

*Daddy wept, "I'm so sorry. I knew better. I'm so sorry."*

*"Toby, run across the street and ask Sharon to come over."*

*Mommy helped Daddy into a neighbor's car, and they left. For six months they were gone, and I shouldered the burden of caring for my younger siblings without thought.*

I knew how bad burns could be. I lived through them. I had learned all the facts. It's not necessarily the burn that kills. The body's natural reaction to trauma is shock, which gives a person the ability to decide between fight or flight. But at the same time, it cuts off blood flow. Shock can kill. The lack of skin allows body fluids to seep out and infection to enter. At the same time, the body is trying to cool down from the burn by sweating. Within a short period of time, the victim becomes dehydrated. A burn victim's body swells to twice its normal size and the body compensates by creating more fluid which causes the kidneys to shut down and closes off breathing passageways making intubation necessary.

Betty needed help but no amount of pleading with the guards brought relief. By morning, she was shaking uncontrollably. Once again, Ms. Johnston on the midnight shift came to the rescue. Betty was taken to the emergency room of the local hospital.

Appalled at the seriousness of Betty's burns, the ER staff called an ambulance to transport her to the burn center in Kansas City. On IV antibiotics and in the ICU for almost a week, Betty's burns, horrid as they were, would not be the last prison-sanctified medical malpractice experienced behind bars. Until life-threatening conditions clearly existed, prison staff ignored emergencies.

Through these experiences, I learned that this inhumane system stopped at nothing to decimate any flicker of light within me. But prison budgets held no room for compassion. Prison profits rely on powerless bedwarmers, people otherwise without value to society.

# 17.

## RUPTURES

**THE LISAS AND I SPENT** the winter crafting our time away.

Lisa mentioned, "Your roommates were so sweet, helping you shower and caring for you after you first broke your leg."

"Yeah, Betty and Faith and Maria are the best. But we have a new roommate now and I'm really struggling with her. She wants prestige and thinks tales of credit card fraud will garner it. Now, she's caught on that I'm not buying it, and since I'm not buying it, nobody else is either, and she blames me."

George commiserated, "That sucks. What're you gonna do?"

"Nothing much I can do. Yesterday she secretly lobbied votes from the pod for her channel on TV then posted a note to the TV while she announced a new rule that what we watched would be elected in advance."

George broke in, "She doesn't have the authority to do that!"

I looked at George, "Of course, she doesn't. She knew that Wednesday night is the only time I watch my show. I swear, she just spends her days dreaming up ways to challenge me."

"Hey, they're changing our rooms into three-person rooms. So we have an opening. You'd have to be in a boat, but still, we'd all be together! You should put in a request," George suggested. But we all knew that moving from one pod to another would be

117

difficult at best, yet I found the idea quite appealing.

"Okay. Time to fly a kite!"

Dr. McCandless saw Lisa as well and reviewed any requests we made. She said, "I don't think you and Lisa would be good together. You both are struggling with the media attention and the high-profile status of your cases. While it's true that you might help lift each other up, there's a chance you might drain each other during the down times making things worse. I can't recommend that you share a cell."

Dr. McCandless's opinion influenced the result of my request. Although I wouldn't be sharing a room with My Two Lisas, the unit team manager offered a compromise. "I do have an opening in a quiet room just a couple of doors down from Lisa, away from the drama in K-Pod. I think it would be a good option B for you."

"Okay, let's do it."

Faith and Betty cried when I told them. Maria had just moved to another room in K-Pod, away from the same woman that troubled me. Maria came to give me a hug; she could relate.

Our nemesis felt sheepish and offered, "Miss Toby, don't move because of me. I'll back off." I lived by a rule to never second guess myself, so I didn't. When I decide, I follow through without looking back. I made the move.

The two Lisas and I spent all our time together, except for when we were locked down. Sometimes I'd see Betty, Maria, or Faith outside, but they rarely left the pod. Betty came to crafts occasionally, but Faith never did. Betty, Maria, and Faith went to church, so I made that a habit too until extremely religious fanatics spoiled the services for Faith and me.

George filled me in a bit more on Lisa's life. The open showers filled Lisa with dread. She didn't want anyone seeing her naked body.

"It's because of her stepdad." George left the reason to my imagination. It wasn't much of a stretch to connect the dots. "At first Lisa refused to shower out in the open, exposed to everyone. But Ms. Wilson started opening our door right after morning count and before the rest of the pod opened. This gave Lisa a chance to shower in an empty pod."

I noticed that except for George and me, Lisa kept to herself. She didn't make friends in the pod. She didn't feel she could trust anyone. Lisa was a woman with a heavy weight hanging over her head.

George focused on her crafts and couldn't be bothered by women who preferred drama and played mind games, but George suffered her own misfortune. The U.S. Marshals arrested her the day before her surgery to remove a tumor in her uterus. She begged and promised that she'd voluntarily turn herself in after surgery, but Lady Justice denied her. Six months passed without medical attention. Her pain grew as did her tumor. George nicknamed the tumor *Lumpy*.

"Lumpy is not behaving today. I can hardly stand up." On the days when Lumpy was good, George joined us walking around the track. She looked nine months pregnant. And then, one day, George collapsed.

Locked down, we watched as they hustled her out of the pod for a trip to the emergency room. Our questions were ignored. A week later, George returned to us.

"Lumpy ruptured. I had to have an emergency hysterectomy. Get this, the doctor told me Lumpy weighed twelve pounds! That's bigger than any baby I ever carried. They didn't think I was going to make it."

Lisa and I listened in horror while George continued, "Toby, they never even called my family. I'm lucky that you thought to call Dad and tell him they'd taken me away. He tracked me down. I'm glad to see you girls again. Not glad to be in this shit hole, though. What are we going to make today?"

As soon as George recovered, both she and her husband were

transferred to a county jail to relieve an overcrowding problem at CCA. Lisa and I grew even closer since it was just the two of us.

One day she said, "Toby, I want to share something with you. I just need to talk to somebody. My lawyer and I discussed it, and he agreed that you're a safe person for me to talk to. I trust you."

Both our court dates were looming, but Lisa faced the death penalty. I still didn't know what I faced because my prosecutor refused to discuss a plea.

Lisa pulled out a medical file. "Here's my MRI. Can you see that white spot there? The doctors say it's a part of my brain that's dead. I think I know how it happened. When I was little, my stepdad beat me. Every day. His favorite thing was to grab my long hair and lift me up and then slam my head onto the concrete. It hurt so bad. He was really mean to me." She sat silently for a few minutes. "I think he killed a part of my brain. Maybe that's part of the reason it happened."

I just sat with her and listened. "Are you scared, Lisa?"

"No, not really. My attorneys are working hard to save my life. I really miss Judy though. I don't know why she left my team. No one's told me anything."

"Do you ever think about it, Lisa?"

Silence.

Lisa looked at the floor. Then she looked away and finally returned her gaze to my face before turning her attention to her hands in her lap.

"I can't let myself go there, Toby. If I did do this terrible thing, what kind of person would that make me?"

# 18.

## UNTESTIMONIED

ONE DAY, OUR POD DOOR popped and in walked George. Lisa and I jumped up and ran to hug her. Gone seven weeks, George eagerly shared her news. "Burt worked out a deal with the feds. He's gonna give information about the suppliers he used in exchange for a ten-year sentence. The best news, as a part of the deal, I get to go home!"

We squealed with delight like a bunch of teenagers with news about the prom. George continued, "I can't wait! Sabrina is only seven years old. She needs me at home. Once they depose Burt, it'll be done."

The first story with a happy ending; perhaps light could be found at the end of CCA.

Two weeks later, George returned from a legal meeting in tears. "Burt has cancer. They've taken him to the hospital. It's bad. I never imagined this. Not in a million years. He hasn't even been sick."

U.S. Marshals took George to the hospital where they removed her handcuffs and let her lay on the bed with him, surrounded by their children, as Burt passed away. George's world imploded. Burt had been her husband and her last chance at freedom. George could hardly believe what happened.

"Toby, he died so suddenly that he didn't have time to take the responsibility for the crime. Without Burt, the feds offered me ten years. Ten years! My Sabrina!" George collapsed in sobs.

This stage of our journeys quickly concluded for the three of us. Lisa's trial loomed, scheduled for October. I would hear the results of my conviction in August, and George knew her fate.

I never quite understood why they call them court *proceedings*. In a dozen or so times to court, I seldom felt that anything proceeded. Strip-searched and shackled, men and women convened at the transport office. Then we were escorted through the parking lot to a transport van. From CCA in Leavenworth, Kansas, the vans made stops in Kansas City, Kansas (KCK) and Kansas City, Missouri (KCMO), each with its own federal courthouse and U.S. Marshals. Inmates waited in basement holding cells for general court times when a marshal escorted them to an elevator connected to a labyrinth of corridors and holding cells for more waiting to be called before a judge.

For me, each court appearance resembled the rest: A marshal escorted me to a table while my attorney, the judge, and a prosecutor discussed my case, after which everyone would stand, while the marshal retrieved me and took me to a holding cell in the basement.

Days with court appearances began at seven o'clock in the morning and ended well after six. Inmates spent the entire time shackled and handcuffed. Plain baloney sandwiches with milk were passed out midday.

Going to court wasted days and exhausted me. Lisa hated court more than I did, but we both faced a relentless media horde which captured and replayed every move and every expression on the evening news before we even returned to CCA.

Attorneys complete an arduous admissions process to be licensed to practice in a federal courtroom. Jim was not licensed for federal court, so I added another attorney to my team.

I'd already added a second to handle my divorce.

Mike in the Federal Public Defenders office became my third representative. Federal attorneys require a lot more money and every woman I knew in the system used a public defender. These federal defenders were excellent lawyers and didn't carry the stigmas of state public defenders. Mike came heaped with praise from Jim and former clients. I couldn't have drawn a luckier hand.

Federal prosecution always wins. Unlike the state justice system, if the feds find you in their crosshairs, prison time becomes certain. There's no beating a federal charge. Border box and presumptive probations don't exist. The feds love to lock people up. They make the whole state process seem like kindergarten. The feds have bottomless budgets; they spare no expense to maximize prison time for each defendant. I swept through the state court process in a matter of weeks, but I would spend almost a year waiting for federal prosecution.

Finally, my attorney Mike brought news of progress, "The judge has ruled that your state and federal sentences are to run concurrently so time you've already served will count toward your federal sentence, as well. Given your charges, the maximum sentence you can get on this federal charge is twenty-seven months."

Since the feds now accepted my state time, twenty-seven months of federal time added only six months more.

"Excellent! Mike, six more months! I can do that." Had I been able to raise my hands I would have cheered.

"I'm requesting twenty-one months. There's a good chance he'll grant my request, so you won't have to do any more than twenty-one months total."

Mike and I faced two choices. Option one: Risk a federal trial, where, like a pit bull, once in their jaws, they tear you up and impose cruel and unusually long sentences; nobody wins a federal trial. Option two: Plead guilty.

The courts—that is, the federal court and the court of public opinion—would never sympathize that I felt compelled to help John Manard. Clearly, of my two choices, only one was viable. The federal process lasted from the first week of October to the very last day of August, eleven full months.

Like a roller coaster, the judge's decision to run my sentences concurrently soared my emotions until the prosecutor delivered another blow. The headlines read, "Federal Prosecutor Seeks Deviation from Sentencing Guidelines for the Dog Lady."

I called Mike. "What does that even mean?"

"She cited extenuating circumstances. I don't know what they are yet, but I will argue against it. We'll have our answer this week."

When the final day arrived, all the previous formalities had been achieved. Mike and I stood before the judge when he asked, "How do you plead?"

I answered, "Guilty as charged, Your Honor."

The judge then eyed a lengthy list of witnesses summoned by the prosecutor, "The defendant has pled guilty. There's no need for more testimony. I'll allow the warden and the marshal," he then addressed the group of witnesses behind the prosecutor, "Thank you for coming. You are excused."

Even so, the prosecutor managed to drag my sentencing out over five long hours; she basked in the media spotlight, citing long-winded justifications for throwing away the keys, but the judge didn't buy it. Yet, to remain objective, he refused Mike's request.

While in a holding cell outside the courtroom, I ate a sandwich. Male inmates, escorted by a marshal, passed by. One said, "Chin up, girl. We're all rooting for you."

The escorting marshal halted the inmates' words of encouragement, hustling them into the elevator, but I'd heard what I needed to hear. Ready to finish my very last court appearance, I assertively ditched the rest of a dry baloney sandwich and warm milk into the trash.

The prosecutor cited and recited more facts and statistics, until finally I was called before the judge. In a clear voice, I stated, "I'm sorry for the harm I caused. I don't have all the answers, but I assure you I will never again be a defendant."

The judge, with his eyes still poring over papers, gave his official ruling, "I don't think Ms. Young is a threat to society, and I doubt she'll ever be in the courtroom again. I don't see cause to deviate from the sentencing guidelines." He then looked over his glasses at me and continued, "Ms. Young, I sentence you to twenty-seven months, the maximum allowed, to be served concurrently with your state sentence of twenty-one months. And I'm going to order that you receive counseling upon release. I'm also ruling that you will be exempt from any drug testing normally ordered for federal parole."

Stacking his papers on his desk, he looked down at me and added, "Ms. Young, you take care of yourself and move past this."

Judge Lindstrom made me feel redeemed and worthy. I would not let him down.

# 19.

## HOPE WITH WHISKERS

**AS IF OUR LAWS AND** the justice system weren't convoluted enough, I discovered the dynamics between state and federal prosecution served only to confuse me further. Although my federal and state sentences ran concurrently, I learned that my first sentence, which happened to be a state sentence, must be satisfied before continuing with the remainder of my federal time. By the time I received my federal sentence, I owed the state only two months more. Perhaps completing my time in federal prison seemed reasonable, since I would soon be transferred to federal prison anyway, but the system often didn't make sense.

Transports came at great cost to inmates. Most inmates suffer a profane depth of poverty. Since personal belongings are not allowed, each relocation forced the repurchase of personal items normally taken for granted. In fact, few could afford to replace what they left behind. I purchased shampoo, deodorant, Chapstick, stamps, paper and pen, tennis shoes, and long underwear, but often waited weeks to receive them.

The day after my federal sentencing, U.S. Marshals summoned me to outtake for processing. "Ms. Young, you're headed back to Topeka to finish your state sentence."

The justice system had shuffled me around so often that I no longer panicked at the prospect of transport. I trusted George to get my radio to Faith; I passed out my commissary items to women who needed them most, packed my personal belongings for my mother to pick up, hugged My Two Lisas, and headed off into the future.

TCF was not home, but it was familiar. No surprises there. I'd spent four months at TCF last year before the federal drama. Eleven months before, I packed my belongings, prison clothes, books, and personal items into a box that waited for me. Extra pounds gifted to me through lack of physical activity at CCA, prevented a good fit. From behind the curtain, I announced, "I need a bigger size."

The inmate assigned to help responded, "I'll make the request. Wear those clothes and take the extras with you. When your request is approved, bring all those clothes back to exchange them for a new size. You'll just have to do the best you can until then."

Stuffed uncomfortably into my clothes, I tottered into the main room, looking more like sausage than an inmate.

Snickering at the sight of me, the worker handed me a brown paper bag. "What's this?" Opening the bag, I peered inside, "Commissary? It must have been delivered the day I left last October to go to CCA. They held it for me?"

The worker nodded. "What else would we do with it?"

"Maybe return it to the commissary stock and refund my money?" With one eye squinted, and a snarl on my face, I reluctantly nibbled on a chip. "Nasty." Perhaps the chips didn't help my problems anyway, so I tossed them in the trash.

Walking back into the maximum custody pod, called I-Max, I sensed a dramatic contrast from my friends back at CCA. Instead of hugs from a cheering circle of women, I felt reduced to little more than inmate number 86519.

"Young, you're upstairs in 206."

I stowed my stuff and took a seat in the dayroom.

"I'm Carly," the woman next to me had bright blue eyes and bouncy hair. She looked my age. "I've been over at minimum custody but I got a write-up so I'm here for a while."

I needed a bit of cheer, so I accepted her invitation to the cafeteria for lunch. A cafeteria beat eating from a tray in my cell. They offered freshly cooked options unlike CCA or the jail, where food was cooked days before and stored on trays in a warming room. TCF had a large garden behind I-Max, which in the summertime brought fresh vegetables to our tables.

Much of the prison drama happened in the cafeteria, so the thirty minutes allowed usually provided some entertainment. The grilled hamburgers and fries served on Saturday nights were a hit.

Carly and I had much in common. Carly enjoyed her mom's support and felt the pain of isolation that incarceration forced on her. Carly's two sons struggled to accept her. College-educated, neither Carly nor I fit the traditional profile of TCF inmates. We spent every minute together that we could.

Carly invited me to a crafting class where we made rubber stamped cards. Nothing as complex or exciting as tatting or quilting, but it killed the time and beat working a jigsaw puzzle alone.

One evening, sitting in my cell before bedtime, I spotted something move.

*It's a mouse! Oh, my goodness. It's so tiny and sweet. I'm going to sneak some bread out of the cafeteria tomorrow and see if he'll come back.*

The next morning on the way to breakfast I shared my secret with Carly. "I have a mouse!"

"They can do something about that if you tell them."

"I want to keep him."

"Keep him?"

"Yep."

"How do we do that?"

"Feed him. I need to sneak some bread back to the pod."

"I'll help!"

Mr. Mouse did return that evening and gobbled up the bread I tossed him.

"Carly! It's working! He'll be eating out of my hand in no time."

The next day at the library, I found an interesting book filled with drawings of flowers and their meanings. Together, Carly and I flipped through the book.

"Rose petal encourages love."

"Pansy encourages compliments and surprise gifts."

"Marigold causes affection, but sometimes accompanied by jealousy."

"Lavender raises spirits. Prevents bad decisions resulting from fatigue or depression."

"Well, that's it, Carly! If we had filled our pockets with lavender, we'd have made better decisions!" I let out a chuckle.

Carly seemed suspicious as a smile crossed her face. Her surprise tickled me more, and I laughed louder. Her eyebrows relaxed, and she began to laugh too. We laughed until our sides ached. That night I decided to make a book for Carly, drawing all the flowers and coloring them with my pencils, writing each flower's meaning on its page.

"I LOVE this, Toby! I will keep it forever."

"Maybe this way you won't forget me—I won't be here long."

"I'll never forget you, Toby. No way."

One day another inmate approached me, "Marcie's going to get you."

"For what?"

"Shuffling your cards too loud."

Carly stared me in the eyes knowingly with a smirk on her face and said, "Maybe we should get some marigolds for Marcie."

We both pealed in laughter.

Marcie's harbinger of doom looked confused, "She can hear you through the wall and it keeps her up in the morning when she wants to take a nap."

We laughed even louder. Most often, prisoners bluffed their way with a bark more menacing than their bite. Like courageous words on a social media post, inmates threatened action until someone called their bluff. Marcie never confronted me.

I enjoyed feeding Mr. Mouse for several weeks until I found him curled in a corner, stiff and unmoving. I rushed to Carly's cell, "Mr. Mouse is dead."

"Oh no! I saw the porters putting out some poison. He must have gotten into it. What are you going to do?"

"Bury him, of course."

"Toby, we can't bury him. They'll see us digging a hole and they'll charge us with escape. Besides, we don't have anything sharp to dig a hole with. You need to flush him."

"I can't flush him; he deserves a proper burial."

"Can't do it, Toby, but if you're gonna try, I'm coming with you. Maybe one of the garden workers could do it for you?"

"I'm not getting into that trap of owing somebody in here." I considered the possibilities and realized I had two, the trash or the toilet. "Okay, Carly, you're right. I'm gonna flush him. It's better than the trash, he wasn't trash." I cradled him up from the floor and upon closer inspection I looked at Carly, "Ummm, Mr. Mouse is Mrs. Mouse."

Carly stood at my door in silence with her head bowed and hands clasped solemnly, as I gently dangled Mrs. Mouse by her tail above the stainless-steel final resting vortex. Mrs. Mouse's tiny eyes were tightly closed, her little hands fisted in grips of death. "I think I'll change my name and move somewhere where nobody knows me and just start over."

Carly opened one eye for a moment, just long enough to see

that Mrs. Mouse waited, dangling above the toilet as I pinched her tail. Carly then closed her eye and offered her best, "Mrs. Mouse lived life to the fullest. She will be missed." Carly paused, then added, "What name would you choose?"

"Sophie—I think. I like Sophie." I dropped Mrs. Mouse as respectfully as a person can drop a dead rodent into a prison toilet, and flushed.

Carly and I watched as the water swirled and sucked away my little friend. I mused, "I'll bet she came inside for the winter to build a nest. Perhaps we could've had babies."

Carly responded, "I like it too. What's your last name going to be?"

"Martin—my mom's maiden name." We both stood over the toilet with prolonged pondering looks.

"Sophie Martin. I like it! When's your release date?"

I replied, "I don't know yet, but I hope I'll still be here on my birthday so Mom and I can share the day. It will be my fiftieth birthday. That's usually a big milestone. Never thought I'd be celebrating this one behind bars."

"Yeah, but look at it this way, it will be your last birthday behind bars!" Carly's eyes opened with a realization, "Hey, my mom is planning a visit. I'll see if she can come that weekend. We can have a party in the visiting room!"

At the same time, we looked up from the toilet at each other and smiled.

Carly asked, "How about a game of cards?"

My prayers were answered. I was still at TCF for my birthday weekend. Carly and her mom sat with us for part of the visit. My heart was full.

On Monday morning I got the call. "Young, pack up."

My state sentence was over. I headed back to federal custody to finish the last six months. Carly cried and promised to stay in touch. "Goodbye Sophie. I'll never forget you!"

And I was off.

*One more step forward. One more piece on this journey, but, for the first time, I can see light.*

# 20.

## LACE UP

NO SUICIDE WATCH AWAITED ME; therefore, processing took place quickly, sending me to J-Pod. Smiling, I danced down the hallway to see My Two Lisas. Strolling like a gold medalist to the awards podium, I pictured a joyous reception, but no Lisas greeted me.

George had been sentenced and shipped out to a prison camp in West Virginia. Nearly a thousand miles from home meant she would receive few, if any, visits from family. Still, she'd prefer a camp over a prison. In the federal camps, inmates had unlimited opportunities for jobs both inside the camp and out. There were no fences to speak of. Although glad George had received camp status, I wished it could have been closer to home.

Lisa's trial had begun as well. In their infinite wisdom, the prison staff and the marshals segregated her from the rest of us. Her crime, trial, and sentence garnered media attention and broadcasts which subjected her to unsolicited conversations and comments from other inmates. CCA administration thought Lisa might fare better in isolation. There wasn't a separate pod for women's seg, so this meant being locked up alone for twenty-three hours a day in one of the J-Pod rooms. They let her out to shower and walk around the pod in the middle of the night when the rest of us were locked down.

Standing at her door or talking to her from the dayroom would get me written up. I spent a lot of time sitting at a table in view of the window in her door and we did our best to communicate without drawing attention.

One day, a new officer that I hadn't seen before during my previous stay, burst into my room. "Young, I'm writing you up for passing contraband to Montgomery."

"What are you talking about?"

"The unit team will be in to discuss it with you."

I knew I hadn't passed anything to Lisa, so I didn't give it heavy thought, but the notion intrigued me. After dinner, my door opened, and a unit team caseworker walked in. "Ms. Young, can you explain this? I'm pretty sure you didn't pass anything to Ms. Montgomery, but I want to hear your story."

I took the card she handed me and laughed, "This is the Mother's Day card I made for Lisa last May. See, it says right on it 'Happy Mother's Day.' Lisa has had that in her possession for months. Long before she was locked down."

"That explains it. This officer didn't know you'd been here before. Don't worry about it. This write-up won't be filed."

I knew a write-up wouldn't matter much, yet I added, "I made it this far clean. I'd like to keep it that way."

The two-person cells in J-Pod had been made into four-person cells. My three twenty-something roommates were new since my last visit to CCA. In fact, a lot of women had moved on. Maria and Betty and Faith were still in K-Pod, but I didn't know anyone in J-Pod at all.

My new roommate, Reggie—doing a five-year sentence—had been called back to Kansas City to testify against her co-defendants who faced life without parole. Hardly beyond her teens, Reggie had been living on her own since the age of twelve and tried to take the GED test several times at the federal prison in Fort Worth. I helped her to develop better study habits and tutored her in math. I longed for the more intellectual conversations I had with friends and family before doing time.

Steve was my very best friend outside of prison. He came to every court appearance and wrote to me daily, even if only a note with a sudoku puzzle in it. He also told me to call collect anytime.

Steve and several other old friends threw lifelines while I drifted in a sea of desperation. They reassured me. They loved me. They reminded me that I mattered. The following letter came at a time when I really needed it:

> *It has to be hard to move on with your life when all of your current activities revolve around one event that happened a year ago. I think being emotional and up and down is very normal for anyone in your position, and also for people that are our age. Midlife seems to be almost as crazy as being a teenager with emotions and pressures.*
>
> *After we talked last night, it occurred to me that you're having trouble adjusting to your time in prison because, in the past, the way that you coped with issues was to throw yourself 100 percent into an activity. It seems to me that you have been avoiding disappointing your family, spouse, kids, friends, co-workers for so long and in the end, you only disappoint yourself.*
>
> *Now you are unable to use your old coping tools— you can only do crafts when you're allowed to, you cannot do crafts 100 percent of the time. My guess is that you would be sewing up a storm if you could, or writing a book, or organizing the prison, or some activity that could be used to consume all your time.*

*You have had to develop new coping skills and not rely on the ones you have used in the past. You have had to turn control of your daily life; when to sleep, eat and have only been allowed a small amount of time for activities.*

*If we are not true to ourselves, at some point a mini or mega meltdown is coming our way. I think you lived through a mega meltdown.*

*I think you get so much press because no one understands why you did what you did, but deep down inside we all understand or at least have felt the silent despair and loneliness in our lives that could drive each of us to our own mega meltdown and we are all afraid.*

*I think it would be a great thing if you could share your story and help others learn to be true to themselves and not try to please everyone else. Show them they need to follow their own dream and not be detoured by other influences that many of us have allowed to impact our life decisions.*

*The beauty of life is that you do not know what is next, you just have to live each day and watch your story unfold.*

*Take care of yourself and keep in mind that life is going to be better and that you will not be in prison forever. You are going to enjoy every day when you complete your sentence, in a way you never have in the past.*

So many people lifted me up during my time behind bars. Friends of my parents sent cards. My aunt sent me her handwritten ten-page Bible study each week. A couple from Toastmasters wrote often and attended every court date. One of them itched to give that horde of reporters a real story but honored my wishes to keep silent. My cousin sent journals and magazines and books and accepted my collect calls. These people outside differed from my cellies.

Of my other two roommates, Tee, wanted to know, "How can I get a divorce?"

I answered, "Well, you just need a lawyer to file the paperwork for you."

Tee hardly let me finish, making me wonder if she even heard me. She continued, "I did somethin' really stupid. I wuz talkin' to this guy while I was locked up in county. He wuz locked up there too. Anyways, we got married by proxy. I don't know nuthin' 'bout him, and I don't wanna be married anyways."

Jaye, looking more like a student than a convict still didn't care to listen as she quickly dumped her story over the top of Tee's, "I was going to college. Doing pretty good too, but the drugs, they got me good. Me and my husband both. Pretty soon we were getting drugs for other people, and I never seemed to show up for classes."

Inmate stories commonly contained three elements. First, most made no point. Regardless of the similarities to countless other stories, I never felt wiser for listening. Second, storytellers never seemed to learn from their own stories, but never tired of interjecting them. Other people's stories just seemed like nuisances, obstacles to telling their story. And third, inmates portrayed themselves as incidental to the crime committed. They never said, "I stole credit cards," instead they said, "I was in the office and the credit cards came up missing."

Jaye and Tee became fast friends and loved the drama brought on by the mixed company found in the pod. The more drama, the better. If boredom struck them just so, they'd create drama.

One day after dinner, before lockdown and evening count, Tee hollered to Jaye, "Lace up!" I looked at Reggie. She responded to my questioning eyebrow, "It means, wear your tennis shoes instead of flip-flops and lace 'em up cuz' there's gonna be a fight."

"A fight? Who's in the fight?"

"We are!" Tee answered. "I'm tired of that room across the way actin' all high 'n' mighty. Me and Jaye are gonna show 'em who's who."

Reggie shrugged at me from her top bunk and then back down at the girls busily lacing up.

Tee looked up. "But, Miss Toby, you ain't in this. You don't know how to fight, better yet just stay out of it altogether. If things start flyin' out there, you come right back in the room and lock the door behind ya."

Jaye added, "She needs to get out of the pod before it even starts. They'll write her up if she's out there cuz she's in our room."

Tee added a solution, "Miss Toby, if we yell PURPLE, you get back to the cell 'cuz it's goin' down."

Kind of excited to be on the inside, I had a ringside seat. I still didn't know the intended targets nor their offense. I walked around the pod warily, but nothing stirred. I was building up this big fight in my head. I thought about all the possible scenarios: Who would win? Would we all get in some kind of trouble, because inevitably they'd want to make an example of us? Would I be implicated simply because I shared a cell with them? What had I become that I felt let down when my cellies didn't fight?

Tee and Jaye were not alone in their prison boredom. Their antics entertained me, and I realized although a fight may have been more exciting, the lack thereof still gave me a lot to think about. I wondered if two years in prison had damaged my character. Had the total absence of production made me lazy?

Had the boredom created within me a superficial sense of entertainment? Had the language of the women around me weakened my love for books? Had the word "felon" become something more than a title on my record? Had prison reduced me to a felon's mindset?

Locked down for the night, I asked, "What happened out there? Or perhaps what *didn't* happen is a better question. I thought it was goin' down."

Jaye muttered, "Wasn't worth it."

The end of the discussion left me, I admit, a tad bit disappointed, yet strangely, I felt accepted. In my cellies' adolescent bravado, I realized we all shared identical circumstances. Yet, what differed was how they viewed themselves. My perspective was changing.

# 21.

## HEARTFELT REASONS

**MANY JOURNALISTS THREATENED ME** during my weakest moments.

"If you don't speak to me, I'll be forced to write a salacious scandal," they would say.

I refused them all.

But one day, I had someone by the name of Kevin Helliker reach out to me. We'd been classmates in high school, but the irony of the Pulitzer Prize under his belt and a prison escape under mine didn't elude me.

Kevin wrote, "Would you tell your story?"

I took a breath while I digested the proposition. Since "No" didn't erupt from my vocabulary, I considered the possibilities. Doing my story justice versus being brought to justice tantalized me.

By this time, God had mixed in me the ingredients necessary to finally handle the moment. I'd been stirred, risen, and kneaded. Prison, like flour on a ball of dough, prevented me from sticking to God's rolling pin.

Kevin's offer struck with perfect timing and tone. He saw my story as nourishment for a hungry world. The front page of the greatest news periodical in the world, *The Wall Street Journal*, reunited us.

Our conversations followed me to CCA where I spent hours talking to Kevin in thirty-minute increments.

People closest to me seemed tired of my story. My attorneys just wanted the highest-level facts. They'd often wave their hands as if trying to brush away annoying cigar smoke, then they'd say, "I don't want to know." My family talked about the weather, or what's for dinner, but they had no ear for the details. Friends (loosely defined) had lives to live. My story boiled within. I felt compelled to tell it.

Kevin talked to John Manard, too, and from bits and pieces of our tale, Kevin crafted a front-page human-interest story, printed in *The Wall Street Journal* nearly two years after the escape. I didn't know it at the time, but his story held the hinge to my future.

Kevin accurately portrayed me, but local reporters in Kansas City disagreed. After many evenings of listening to stories about the crazy Dog Lady, I walked back to my room and announced, "Kansas City's gossip and finger-pointing has convinced me it's about time to move."

My roommates nodded, "But, where?"

Tee suggested, "Maybe Santa Fe, New Mexico?"

"Noooo," Jaye and Reggie objected.

Jaye then said, "Chicago?"

I replied, "Nope. How about Boston?"

At the same time, all three said, "Boston!"

Reggie said, "That's it; that's where you need to go, Boston!"

Boston intrigued me. I felt pulled. I'd decided that John Manard and I should go to Boston when we left Tennessee during the escape, but I didn't know why.

The very next day, Monday morning, I received a FedEx overnight envelope… from Boston. No one had heard of getting a FedEx delivery inside prison.

An officer delivered it to me directly saying, "I have to watch you open it." This could be no coincidence.

My roommates spoke at once, urging me to open it.

Stunned that they gave it to me, I obliged them. I tore open the package, pulled out the correspondence and scanned the content.

"It's a job offer. From some guy—Alden—in Boston, who read the article in *The Wall Street Journal*. He says he'll 'champion me with the parole board' if I agree to work for him. He needs a website built and sees the article in the paper as an opportunity for us both."

The officer smiled and took the empty FedEx package, leaving me with the letter.

"Are you going to write back?"

"Nope, even better. He gave me his phone number and said to call collect." I marched out of the cell and headed for the phone on the wall across the pod. I dialed the number in the letter, it rang.

My heart pounded, Alden answered politely, "Hello, Toby. I've been expecting your call. This is Alden."

"Hello, Alden. You won't believe it, but I decided just last night that I wanted to move to Boston when I get out of prison. Talk about perfect timing!"

Alden seemed polite and professional, no-nonsense; he got straight to the point, "Toby, I have an idea for a new type of social sharing system. I entered this idea in a contest, but should I lose the contest, I intend to fund it personally. I know you'll need to get a job to meet the requirements of your parole, and I also know it can be hard to find one that's decent. If you're willing to move to Boston, I'd like to offer you a job as a project manager and web designer on my team."

I followed Alden's lead quickly cutting through the chaff, "That sounds exactly like the kind of work I love doing, and I'd love to live in Boston. Of course, we'll have to talk more, and both my state and federal parole officers will have to buy in. You can talk to them more and answer whatever questions they might have. I'm sure we'll have plenty of time to talk in the next three months before final decisions are made." I couldn't help but smile inwardly, the conversation reminded me of the heady days when I ran teams of development staff at the Sprint campus.

"Great! I'll contact the parole board, both in Kansas and Massachusetts and set things in motion. I'm going to have a laptop and cell phone sent to your mother's house so you can start working immediately upon release. If it doesn't work out, or you decide not to come, you can just return the equipment by mail. If you plan to come, though, I'd like you here within thirty days of being released."

"The rest will be up to my parole officers. I'll come as soon as the paperwork is ready."

"Call me collect any time. You have my number."

After two years immersed in the dark world of prison, Alden's offer burned brightly. My future arrived bearing gifts—that is until my sisters chimed in by phone about the story, "I don't like it at all. Nobody is happy with this. Why can't you just do your time? Why the need to talk about it? We're sick of hearing it all again and again and again. We all know you went to prison—the whole world knows. Why bring it up over and over? Can't you just get past it?"

My brother, Tom, one of few allies, grew weary from the sisters' complaints, "I wish you'd never done the story, Toby. Maybe it would have been better to just stay quiet."

I had expected Kevin's article to help the world understand, but my family's reactions cast doubt. The Wall Street Journal was not circulated inside the prison, so I flew blindly. I had no idea what my sisters meant—what did Kevin write? I made a phone call. "Kevin, what in the world is in this article? I have furious sisters and a job offer. It must be some kind of story."

"Oh! I totally forgot you have no way to read it. Here, let me get my copy and I'll read it to you."

## The Heart Has Its Reasons

By KEVIN HELLIKER

For 46 years, Toby Phalen Young was a model of propriety.

Married to her high-school sweetheart since the age of 20, Ms. Young was a respected mother, business professional and philanthropist. She found homes for stray dogs and did volunteer work at a prison. She never even got a traffic ticket. Her siblings called her "goody two shoes."

Almost exactly two years ago, however, on the eve of Valentine's Day, Ms. Young used her volunteer status at Lansing Correctional Facility to smuggle out a convicted murderer. At age 27, John Manard had convinced the 48-year-old Ms. Young of his undying love for her. Before running off with him, she withdrew $42,000 from her retirement plan, purchased a getaway vehicle and packed it with her belongings. Her husband found a pair of pistols missing from their home, a discovery that turned the fugitive lovers into America's most-wanted couple.

The escape brought a parade of journalists into this blue-collar town across the river from glittering Kansas City, Mo. But nobody here could or would offer insight into the sudden wild streak of a community pillar who lived down the street from her parents in the only town she'd ever called home.

Even after federal authorities located the fugitives in a honeymoon cabin in Tennessee, Ms. Young's friends and loved ones reserved judgment. Many were convinced she had fallen under the spell of a manipulator at a vulnerable time, when her father was dying and Ms. Young herself was recovering from cancer.

"In the middle of a mid-life crisis, she got caught in the trap of a no-good rotten con artist," says Michael Peterson, a state legislator here who has known Ms. Young's family, the Phalens, since the 1950s. Add her attorney, Michael Harris: "Toby is lucky not to be lying in a ditch in Appalachia with a bullet in her head."

Yet in Ms. Young's account, the first she has offered publicly since her arrest two years ago, Mr. Manard didn't wrong her and never would have. "Everybody wants me to hate him, but I don't," she says, visibly embarrassed to be sitting on the inmate side of plexiglass, a telephone pressed to her ear.

Her guilty pleas to felony charges in state court in 2006 and federal court last year offered no insight into the motivation behind her crimes, and she never provided any to the media -- in part, she says, for fear no one would understand. She cites a quote, from French philosopher Pascal, that she recently came across in prison, where she reads a book a day: "The heart has its reasons that reason knows nothing of."

Her husband of 28 years, a fire captain named Pat, has rejected all requests for interviews. For this article, he declined to return calls placed to his home, his cell phone and his place of work. "I want to assure you that no matter what may come of this, it will remain a private and personal matter," Mr. Young said in a statement to the media following Ms. Young's arrest.

In a prison cell elsewhere in Kansas, meanwhile, Mr. Manard professes his love for her. "I miss her so much, I'd have to wipe out an entire rainforest to put it on paper," he said in a recent letter to *The Wall Street Journal*.

The felonies that cost Ms. Young her home, marriage, financial security and freedom might never have occurred if she had shared her unhappiness with someone other than an inmate seeking to woo her. But she had lived her life according to a family credo, she says: "Phalens don't complain. Phalens suck it up."

Even by those standards, Ms. Young's father, James Phalen, stood out. At age 27, he nearly died in a fire that burned off his ears and hospitalized him for six months. Upon discharge, he could barely move his arms, so tight was his scalded flesh. Returning to his job as a machinist at the railroad, however, he didn't seek work that would accommodate this limitation. Instead, he sought the most-hated job on his shift -- crawling under an engine and reaching up to replace its brake shoes -- for the purpose of painfully forcing that skin to stretch. It was a story he sometimes told when he heard his children complaining.

Of the seven Phalen children, none took it to heart more than the oldest, Toby. "'Great' was the only answer Toby ever gave to 'How's it going?'" says her youngest sister, Amy Phalen, an Arkansas housewife.

At the Catholic high school where her grandmother had been a teacher and her father a football standout, Ms. Young is still remembered as the pep-club president, a straight-A student and the steady girlfriend of a baseball star named [Rob]. A good-looking kid from a troubled part of town, Pat hung out so often in the Phalen house that Toby's younger siblings say they considered him a brother. "Shy, quiet, polite," is how Ms. Phalen, Toby's sister, describes her former brother-in-law, whom she says she loves.

At age 20, Pat and Toby married. Of the 200 members of the Bishop Ward High class of 1975, dozens married their high-school sweethearts. These unions in part reflected a belief in church teachings: When a Bishop Ward couple started thinking about having sex, marriage was the right thing to do. And among her siblings, Toby was known as fanatical about doing the right thing. "She was less like a sister than like a third parent," says Ms. Phalen.

Pat became a fireman, Toby a secretary. They bought a house not far from her parents and had three children within seven years. The middle child, their only daughter, died a few hours after birth.

Ms. Young says her method of handling that setback, and hardship generally, was to stay busy. While raising two sons and working full-time, she attended college at night and obtained two undergraduate business degrees. She landed a job at Sprint Corp., where she became a project manager specializing in systems analysis. "Toby figured out a way to make any process more efficient," says Steven Smith, a tax expert who worked with Ms. Young on several projects at Sprint.

In 2001, she was earning a six-figure income as a member of a project at Sprint called ION, an attempt to bundle telephone and Internet services. But the attacks of 9/11 rocked the economy at a time when Sprint was already reeling from the failure of its proposed merger with MCI WorldCom Inc. In October 2001, Sprint killed the ION project and laid off most of ION's work force, ending Ms. Young's 14-year career at the company.

Reeling from the loss of her executive dreams, she bounced around: She started a Web-design venture with her 20-something son, enrolled in nursing school, began working part time at a veterinary clinic. Then a lump on her neck turned out to be thyroid cancer. In March of 2004, she underwent surgery.

This glimpse of her mortality evoked in her a desire for meaningful work, and her mind turned to dogs. Rescuing, training and showing dogs had been a life-long avocation.

At the veterinary clinic where she worked, she became aware of the large number of strays around Kansas City that got exterminated for lack of adoptive owners. So she broached the idea of starting a dog-adoption service.

A fellow clinic employee, whose husband worked at Lansing Correctional Facility, a nearby state prison, suggested Ms. Young consider using prisoners to train stray dogs. Around the country, so-called cell-dog programs had been shown to reduce inmate violence and convert doomed canines into adoptable pets.

A visit to the warden's office at Lansing Correctional Facility convinced Ms. Young the idea would work. Going onto the Internet, she downloaded the documents needed to create a non-profit, which she called the Safe Harbor Prison Dog Program. She enlisted volunteers and raised money. Within a year, the program trained and found homes for nearly 700 strays.

These penitentiary pooches became famous across the Midwest, attracting dog seekers to the suburban Kansas City PetSmart store where Ms. Young held adoption fairs on weekends. Violence diminished inside the prison, officials said, in part because many inmates wanted to share their cells with a dog, and obtaining one required good behavior.

The program brought a new kind of publicity to an institution known for four decades as the harsh setting of Truman Capote's "In Cold Blood." In media outlets ranging from television and talk radio to newspapers and pet publications, the dog program generated coverage that made prison officials look progressive and hardened criminals humane. "Part of your heart goes into each dog," Leslie Ellifritz, a convicted murderer and rapist, told the Associated Press.

The publicity turned Ms. Young into one of Kansas City's highest-profile nonprofit executives. In animal-control circles, she became known as a savior. "Toby took the lame, the ugly, the dogs nobody else wanted," says Karen Sands, shelter director of the Humane Society of Greater Kansas City.

But privately, she was coming unglued. The sense of well-being she'd always received from striving non-stop eluded her now, she says, and in an attempt to regain it, she worked all the harder. When she wasn't collecting strays or training inmates or updating her Web site with photos of adoptable canines, she was writing her weekly newsletter or cleaning the kennel behind her house, where 15 or so dogs awaited transfer to prison.

Yet staying busy no longer warded off a sense of despair and alienation, Ms. Young recalls. Her achievements -- no matter how celebrated -- seemed inadequate to her, because thousands of local dogs continued to be exterminated each year. Behind the wheel of the Safe Harbor cargo van, she says she increasingly found herself battling the impulse to steer into oncoming traffic.

Only during visits behind bars did she find any relief. In a fortress packed with men, her appearance at age 47 drew more compliments than she'd received at 27, and not just from inmates. One guard, she says, always greeted her by saying, "Hey, beautiful." Inmates worshipped her for being able to place a dog in their cells.

In particular, she enjoyed her dealings with Mr. Manard, partly, she says, because he challenged her. Early on, he good naturedly questioned her argument that positive reinforcement, rather than discipline, produced the best trained pets. But after agreeing to eliminate "no" from his dog-handling vocabulary, he became an ace, she says, his charges exhibiting good behavior and happy dispositions long after adoption.

Mr. Manard says he loved handling menacing beasts, such as an American bulldog named Kane, that entered prison snarling and left licking hands.

In his first interview on the subject of their courtship and escape, Mr. Manard says he never imagined Ms. Young would take interest in him. "I respected her -- she was like Mother Teresa -- and I was careful not to cross any lines," said Mr. Manard, in a collect call from a maximum-security cell in El Dorado, Kan.

Ms. Young says Mr. Manard began offering tips on how to handle this guard, that inmate or some logistical problem. She says she watched him defuse tension between inmates. "Like a great corporate manager, he could turn people his way without creating resentment, by persuading them that his idea was theirs," she says.

Mr. Manard says he marveled at her innocence. At age 47, she told him she'd never been drunk, smoked a cigarette, tried drugs or watched pornography -- lines he had crossed by 14, at which age he was living in a juvenile detention center, he says. A tattoo across his torso said: "Hooligan."

But by age 27, he was different, he told her. Behind bars, he'd obtained his high school equivalency diploma, taught himself to play several instruments and joined a prison band. He eventually won release to medium-security from maximum-security status. "His disciplinary history had improved from the time that he was first incarcerated," says Bill Miskell, spokesman for the Kansas Department of Corrections, noting that Mr. Manard "qualified for the privilege to participate" in the dog program. At the time, about 70 of the prison's nearly 2,500 inmates were involved in that program.

Yet Mr. Manard suspected no amount of reform would ever win him freedom, he told Ms. Young. At age 17 he'd received a life sentence for his role in a carjacking that left a passenger fatally shot. By Mr. Manard's calculations, the earliest he would gain parole would be 2028, and he felt certain he wouldn't win it even then. His biggest fear, he says, was that he'd be buried on prison grounds.

All this, he told Ms. Young, for a crime he never committed. As an adolescent, he says he'd been a "self-centered adrenalin junkie," and not because his parents hadn't taught him right from wrong. "My life wasn't taken from me -- I gave it away [by] stealing the guy's car," he says.

Yet he says he didn't shoot anybody. He hadn't even been carrying a gun, he says, asserting that his older accomplice accidentally pulled the trigger. "I would never kill anyone," Mr. Manard told her.

Paul Morrison, the prosecutor in the case, says he believes that Mr. Manard didn't pull the trigger. But he says that the felony-murder law in Kansas renders that issue irrelevant, because Mr. Manard participated in a crime that clearly had the potential to turn violent. Prosecutors say felony murder, besides being a deterrent, avoids the legal gridlock that occurs when defendants endlessly point fingers at each other.

Felony murder is a concept that many other nations -- and some American states -- have abolished as unfair. Going online, Ms. Young researched the subject and concluded Mr. Manard had a point. "If you didn't kill anybody, you shouldn't be convicted of murder and sent to prison for life," she says.

Sympathy also flowed the other way. Mr. Manard could tell she was unhappy, she says, and his concern was particularly helpful when her father, a loving and powerful figure in her life, was diagnosed with cancer in

2005. Mr. Manard also asked about her marriage: Why was she spending 50 hours a week inside a prison?

Ms. Young says she replied that nearly 30 years of marriage had created a bond between her and her husband that wasn't measurable in hours-per-week spent together. "He's the only man I ever dated," she said, reciting an oft-rehearsed line that she thought sounded romantic.

For years a spinner of fictitious tales of domestic bliss, Ms. Young recalls a letter she wrote regaling relatives with the story of a salsa-making fiasco that dissolved in laughter between her and her husband. "It never happened," she says. "But it was how I wished our marriage was." Instead, she felt the marriage was bereft of affection.

On occasion, she broached the subject of divorce, but says her husband laughed and said she had nothing to complain about. He never hit her, wasn't a drunk and didn't cheat, she says. He brought home a fire-captain's salary. She suspected such factors would sway her parents and siblings, who regarded Mr. Young as a son or brother.

"I didn't see any way out," she says.

At the prison, Mr. Manard endlessly asked her: "What's wrong?" Often, she answered that she felt obliged to please too many people, including her husband. Gradually, she confided her marital woes. Mr. Manard suggested that she obtain one of those bracelets that say "WWJD," for "What Would Jesus Do?" Instead of Jesus, however, Mr. Manard suggested that she ask herself, "What would John do?"

In times of stress, Ms. Young says she started asking herself that.

He began wooing her. When he raved about the way her hair color matched her eyes, the creaminess of her skin, her taste in clothes, "it was like water on a dying plant," she says.

A turning point in their relationship came in October 2005, both say, when an inmate threatened her.

After that, Ms. Young says she refused to return without protection. She says an officer in the warden's office responded by appointing Mr. Manard her unofficial protector. "He said John would accompany me everywhere I went inside," she says.

Prison officials acknowledge Ms. Young reported a threat. But Mr. Miskell, the state corrections department spokesman, says prison officials didn't -- and never would -- appoint an inmate to protect a volunteer or visitor.

No one disputes that the two spent hours together or that Ms. Young had extraordinary access inside the prison. When two of her sisters came along one day, they quickly insisted on leaving, alarmed to find themselves surrounded by inmates without a guard nearby, recalls Ms. Phalen, Toby's sister. Ms. Young's former Sprint colleague, Mr. Smith, had a similar reaction when he tagged along with her to inmate cells, no guard in sight.

"Frankly, it kind of freaked me out," says Mr. Smith, who provided tax services to the dog program. "I told Toby, 'I'm not coming back.'"

Mr. Miskell, the corrections department spokesman, says, "People who tour facilities for the first time are often taken off-guard by the amount of movement and interaction between inmates and others." He says those who work or volunteer in a correctional facility must meet necessary training requirements, as Ms. Young did.

In rare moments of solitude behind bars, Ms. Young and Mr. Manard professed their love. He told her he wanted to be with her every day, forever. She told him that she'd never felt this way about anybody, that just talking with him fulfilled something vital in her. In December of 2005, he asked whether Ms. Young would run off with him, if he managed to escape?

"I would," she replied.

Mr. Manard says he asked that as a joke, but her reply turned escape into an obsession. He focused his thoughts on fitting into a box. Stretching himself to become more limber, and dropping nearly 30 pounds to a weight of 155, Mr. Manard tried without success to squeeze his 6-foot-2-inch frame into the box. But one night, he says, he dreamed of a way to pretzel into it. Trying it the next morning, he found it worked.

Originally, both say, he was determined to mail himself out of prison. But she argued that plan would never work. Getting past the gates was unlikely, since a heart-beat detector is generally applied to cargo trucks. Then Mr. Manard broached the idea of sneaking out in Ms. Young's van, which often didn't undergo heart-beat detection.

His plan: When she pulled up to collect dogs, Mr. Manard would be hiding in the box, inside a dog crate that also contained food bowls and other supplies. The inmates who always loaded dog crates into the van would -- unknowingly, he said -- load him into her van. Then the two would flee for parts unknown.

Ms. Young says she agreed to the plan without allowing herself to consider the consequences. As laid out, it seemed to involve minimal complicity on her part, she says. "I wouldn't be loading him into the van. I'd just be pulling up to collect dogs the way I always did on Sunday morning," she says.

As part of the plan, she drained $42,000 from her retirement plan, bought a 1997 Chevrolet pickup as a getaway vehicle and hid it in a rented storage unit.

Using a contraband cellphone inside prison, Mr. Manard rented a cabin in rural Tennessee. In the month before their breakout, he and Ms. Young communicated 12,000 minutes by phone, she says. One morning, Ms. Young says, her husband fished her vibrating phone from her purse and found a text message that read: "good morning, baby. I love you."

"That's a wrong number," Ms. Young told her husband.

She says her husband responded that he didn't consider her sexually capable of having an affair.

On the afternoon of Sunday, Feb. 12, the phone rang in the home of Ms. Young's parents. Peggy Phalen, Ms. Young's mother, recalls being told that an inmate was missing from prison and Ms. Young had failed to show at that morning's adoption fair at Pet-Smart. Terror struck that she'd been taken hostage. "We prayed for the best but feared the worst," she says.

Within hours, though, evidence of Ms. Young's complicity emerged -- her missing belongings, the money taken out of her retirement fund -- and by Valentine's Day, federal authorities were calling her role incontrovertible.

In Tennessee, meanwhile, the fugitives spent Valentine's Day in their cabin, exchanging gifts: She bought him a bass guitar. He bought her a parakeet, that he named Lynyrd, a reference to Lynyrd Skynyrd's song, "Freebird." They made love, talked for hours, and planned outings. On Feb. 24, they toured an aquarium, and saw an IMAX movie about lions and stopped at Barnes & Noble, where Mr. Manard bought Ms. Young one of his favorite books, "Where the Red Fern Grows," a tale of a boy who trains hunting dogs.

After they left the bookstore, authorities spotted them. Following a short chase, they were arrested.

As the image of Ms. Young, handcuffed and bewildered, flashed across TV screens around the nation, her husband refused to utter any public criticism of her. His subsequent request for an emergency divorce didn't cite grounds. A judge here quickly granted it.

In a letter to a Kansas City television station, Mr. Manard described his 12 days with Ms. Young as the high point of his life. Even after receiving an extra decade of prison time for the escape, Mr. Manard says in an interview that it was worthwhile.

"I got to meet an angel who for some reason graced me with her love," he says.

Lost amid the weepy guilty pleas of Ms. Young was what happened immediately after the escape. She and Mr. Manard stopped at her home, so that she could place in her backyard kennel the adoption-ready dogs in her van. She says she knew other volunteers in the prison program would find homes for the dogs. "After rescuing them once, I wasn't going to ditch them in a field," she says.

While she was unloading the dogs, Mr. Manard -- who was supposed to be hiding in the front of the van -- says he slipped into the house and grabbed a pair of handguns. Ms. Young says she never wanted to bring the guns or even touched them. ("I hate guns. I'm 100% for gun control," she says.) But federal prosecutor Terra Morehead says that even if this story were true, which she doubts, it wouldn't diminish Ms. Young's guilt.

Her 27-month sentence forced Ms. Young to ponder the damage her betrayal wrought upon loved ones, including her grown sons, one of whom she says hasn't spoken to her since her arrest. Her father died two months later, after granting her forgiveness, she says. "I've told Toby that her father may have died sooner because of what she did, and she just has to live with that," says her mother, a retired Catholic-college administrator who visits Ms. Young weekly in prison.

Upon completing her sentence this May, Ms. Young says she expects the repair of shattered trust with loved ones to take a while. She plans to live with her mother and wants to work at a bookstore.

She doesn't miss the life she lost, she says, asserting that the humiliation and deprivations of prison have been beneficial. Long dismissive of psychotherapy, she now praises the prison therapists who, initially placing her on suicide watch, began treating her for depression.

She refuses to endorse the theory that she is the brainwashed victim of a self-serving convict. She says she believes John Manard loved her, that he escaped to be with her, that he is a reformed man worthy of freedom. When legally able to make contact with him, she says she will do so.

Her deepest regret is that his lengthened sentence may keep him behind bars for life. Her voice breaking, she says, "I wonder if he'd be better off if he'd never met me."

"Kevin, I like it. I think it sounds true and accurate."

Kevin replied, "Thanks. Everyone who's read it likes it. In fact, my brother thinks you're a hero."

I laughed. "A hero. Well, that's a first. Maybe I should join your family."

After hearing Kevin read the story, my family's reaction puzzled me more. In my darkened room, I wondered what I could do to appease my sisters.

*Do they hate the story because it makes me seem like a real person?*

*Maybe they're upset about it because now the world has an insight into who I was, how I was thinking. Maybe the picture Kevin painted wasn't the cruel and evil person they'd like to believe I am. Maybe now they have a harder time playing victims of my crime.*

*Maybe my sisters truly, really, deep down, don't love me at all. Maybe they never did. They will never ever forgive me. I will forever be branded by the sisters as an evildoer who killed our father and is of no value to the family at all, a sister that hangs a stone around their collective necks, drowning them from the life they envisioned for themselves.*

*Can they not let go of the embarrassment? Can they not be proud that I'm rising out of this despair? Maybe, what they can't handle is a window into my life so readers could understand my thoughts because, somehow, it weakens theirs.*

*Are they secretly afraid that if I had broken so catastrophically that it's possible they might too? Do they see their own vulnerabilities in my actions? What kind of love tries to destroy someone who's trying to find her way out of darkness? Would they have liked it better if I'd died in that car crash?*

Suddenly, it all made sense.

*Being killed would have been an easier pill to swallow. People would have rushed in to support them in their loss. Instead, they feel like the world is pointing at them, wondering. Yes, they wish I was dead. That would be easier for them all to handle. What they can't handle is an awakened Toby. Death... Was it better? Maybe. How can I do it? Can I die from taking too many thyroid pills?*

Reaching out for the last lifeline I had left; I asked an officer to take me to Dr. McCandless immediately.

# 22.

# ON THE THIRD DAY

**THE TIME HAD COME TO DEAL** with my past, my insecurities, my demons. Blind to the future, I saw no reason to continue. Kevin's article exposed my broken soul to the world. I couldn't control how my sisters behaved or felt about *The Wall Street Journal* article, much less how they felt about me. I could hardly control my own feelings.

Perhaps the article dredged up feelings they weren't ready to face. My shameful voluntary part in the escape disgraced my family, but broken people need love. I used the article to cry for help. John Manard's love offered me, for the first time, a contrast to four decades of festering neglect.

A sick whisper shouted accusations, "Killing yourself would be a noble act of love for your sisters."

Twisted, venomous, murder-words laced with tiny elements of logic and beauty warped my mind, deceiving me. Suicide seemed easy and quick, maybe the only way out. The consideration haunted me. I turned my darkened gaze up from the pit to the doctor.

Dr. McCandless watched me closely from her side of the desk. "What's going on, Toby?"

"They're all mad at me because I gave an interview."

"I read that story last weekend. I thought it was a good story. It sounds like you've started to work things out."

"My sisters wish I'd died rather than gotten arrested."

"You don't know that for sure."

"Maybe not, but I know it for pretty sure. They think I killed our dad. They hate me. Now, I doubt they ever loved me."

"Tell me more."

"What if they're right? What if the world would be better if I was gone? It would make their lives easier for sure."

She raised a questioning eye at me. I sat staring at the floor with my chin buried against my chest. My cheeks wet, hair bedraggled, my mind, distant from my violated reality, wandered, and wondered, *Could an overdose of thyroid meds kill me?*

"I'm thinking maybe suicide watch is a good option for you. It's Friday. Maybe you could take the weekend to ponder things without the drama. Think of it as a cocoon, a safe place to find yourself."

"I never thought I'd say this, but I think that's exactly what I need."

In my head, every thought chased and danced and swirled with a question mark.

*Why? What's the purpose? What good can come from this mess? Nobody wants me. I'll never get out. Where will I go? I'll just be a pariah, drifting around the country with no roots. Please, God, please, can't you just take me? I'm ready to go.*

For the entire first day, suicide spoke.

*You're no good. Your family would rather you die. The world has no use for a loser like you. Do it! Just get it over with. Do it already. We're tired of waiting.*

I just lay there. The voice got more insistent.

*Who do you think you are? Everyone knows you're a felon. That's right. Felon. Forever branded. Felon. Felon. Felon. Felons are nobodies. They exist in the shadows. You're doomed to that shadowy* life. *Nobody cares if you live or die. You are nothing and the pain IS unbearable. DO IT! Death is too good for you, but it would be better than this.*

The voices, like flames in my head, were given the power to dismiss my intangible values.

*The world would be better without me.*

I thought about my romance-less marriage and all those wasted years. Twenty-eight years I could never get back.

*Why is the only way out such a drastic one?*

My mind opened wide when I realized those twenty-eight years were a prison too.

*My sons. Why don't they love me anymore? Will they ever talk to me again? Why don't they write back? Why does Rob think it's best for them to stay away?*

And then I realized: He won.

*Rob won. This was the only way he could pull my sons away from me. They weren't the real prize—punishing me was. Does that mean I've lost? After all this, am I nothing but a loser?*

Shame raged, slimy black and green. With death my best option, I cared not about love. I had been relieved of duty. The massive decompressions pushed me beyond breaking, to a cold, catatonic state. My inner five-year-old took nourishment and power from fear, approval, love, and anxieties; but this event, void of emotion, didn't trigger my little superhero coping mechanism. Suicide had become a real threat, a permanent solution to a temporary problem.

*Can I bring focus back to this moment and move past it? Find a way to resolve it?*

The day slipped into evening. A unit team member stopped by. "I called your mom and told her you didn't want any visitors tonight."

"That's not true. I do want my mom, just not my sisters."

"Well, you can't have visitors on suicide watch."

"I know, but you could have told her the truth."

"We can't let your family know you're on suicide watch. That's policy."

"Well, it's a stupid policy. I think my family should know if I'm struggling. My poor mom will think I'm mad at her or I don't want to see her."

*Perhaps my suicide would hurt Mom. Could I do that to her? She doesn't deserve that either. But it still seems to be my best option.*

Saturday, I felt glued to the floor, eyes closed, replaying scenes in my head, trying to see a path to a future. Many years of ignored stress bubbled to the surface.

Once again Dad's nightmare filled my mind.

*Daddy planned to burn the freshly cut willow branches, but they were green and wouldn't catch easily. Embers from the previous night's fire smoldered in the bottom of the big steel drum. He poured fuel over the branches, and, in a split second, an unexpected inferno towered above the barrel. Startled, he jumped back and spilled fuel on his face and shoulders. It was an ever-so-slight lapse in judgment that morphed into an event that ignited Daddy's head and shoulders.*

*Fire arcing red sucked away Daddy's oxygen and consumed his clothes, hair, and future. Daddy dropped to the ground and rolled; flames whirled around his head like an unquenchable demon.*

*When Daddy finally killed the fire, he lived.*

*Daddy's backyard battle sent shockwaves for generations. The gravity of that event was immeasurable. No longer a five-year-old princess playing under the weeping willow tree, I bore the brunt of urgency, desperation, and anxiety; these powerful emotions gushed over me. The fire that scarred Daddy's face also scarred my heart.*

*The terror struck by Daddy's appearance faded, yet the spirit that followed him up those basement steps haunts me still. It set in motion a lifetime of denial, given over to a choking sense of duty. To survive, I needed different eyes to see my new upturned world. The day Daddy left for the hospital; an unhealthy work ethic took hold. Not only did I unfairly assume duties as a five-year-old caretaker, but I also buried emotions as my way of coping.*

*For many reasons, a five-year-old little girl whispered through the flames, "You're not free to dance and dream until the work is done."*

*I lost Daddy's secure embrace and assuring smile. I lost the dad who was always quick to tell me my brown eyes were dazzling, or that my orange and pink dress was his favorite too. More urgent than foolish dreams of castles, giggling, and kite strings, the clock compelled me to get things done—no time to play.*

*As my mind and body rose to life's challenges, that little girl, like an orphaned child within me, took the brunt of stressful crises, yet remained mired in a sea of misconceptions, loss, and need. The consequences of that day pushed me to produce.*

*I tried to shelter my siblings from the same uncertainty. Unasked, I assumed a mother's duty and took care of those babies. I changed diapers, washed dishes, fixed sandwiches, and did whatever I could to ease Mom's burdens.*

*I mistook urgency for maturity and drove myself to perform for anyone that had a need. And everyone needed me. My siblings needed me. Mommy and Daddy needed me. In the shadow of everyone's need, a fracture widened and separated me from my childhood. The abandoned child took care of everyone and remained suspended in time as the clock ticked on while I strangled a lifetime, shouldering a duty that was never mine to fill.*

*In 1963, hospital visitors had to be at least fourteen years old, no exceptions, which meant none of us saw Daddy during his six-month hospital stay, a lifetime in the mind of a five-year-old. Nobody could convince us he was ever coming home. The image in my mind of Daddy faded to a soft, warm, long-ago feeling.*

*Skin grafts, peeling, painful treatments, medications, morphine addiction, infections, and dozens of life-threatening crises ensued. Finally, the doctors exhausted all the medical help they could provide. It was time for him to go home.*

*They warned Mom, "Perhaps the biggest battles still lie ahead. Your husband will battle depression. Yet the only chance to achieve a normal life begins once the burn victim goes home to the life they left behind." Dad faced once-simple activities that he could no longer do.*

*Mom, in the first year of Dad's recovery, sustained a lifetime of hardships. Her grieving children and dying husband needed her desperately. Sixty miles from home, she lifted Dad's spirits, sometimes providing his only purpose. Day after day, for months, our hearts broke as she peeled one child off her leg, while gently pushing away another so she could leave for the hospital. We ached to be with her, but with tears streaming down her face, she knew we all had only one chance. Daddy must live.*

*Short of any income whatsoever, we survived on handouts and the generosity of others. At only twenty-five, Mommy emerged as our surrogate superhero.*

*After overcoming insurmountable odds, Mom feared we might reject Daddy. At twenty-seven, just before the willow tree tragedy, Daddy resembled a young Paul Newman. And ten years before, he'd been the athletic superstar of his high school. At six feet tall and 200 pounds, his chiseled chin and blond hair turned heads.*

*One afternoon, the door opened unexpectedly. Mom appeared, supporting a shadow of a man, a stranger. At barely 128 pounds, Daddy's frail body and twisted skin couldn't extinguish the fire in his eyes.*

*"Daddy!" I couldn't hold back the squeal in my voice.*

*"Kids…" Daddy cried.*

*The sound of his voice made our world right again. Daddy may have lost some physical prowess, but he returned with a spiritual gift, an understated strength, and a resolve to be our world again. That inner glow outshone the physical looks he'd had before, making him beautiful in an entirely new way. He returned the superhero I always knew he was.*

*Despite seeming perfect to us, Daddy was barely able to care for himself. The scar tissue under his arms bound them to unnatural movements. In the hospital, nurses had served his every need. They brought him water to sip and helped him walk to the bathroom, but Mommy had her hands full with five active children and didn't have time to coddle him. She simply couldn't take on caring for a sixth child without help.*

*At her breaking point, when Daddy asked for a drink of water, she followed the doctor's advice, "Jim, I don't have time to take care of you. I'm not your private nurse. If you can't get your own glass of water, you'd better just go back to the hospital."*

*Dad was crushed. Mom didn't want to hurt him, but she needed him back as the head of the family. With poise, Mom escaped to the basement where she cried privately.*

*When she returned to the living room, Dad waited for her. "Peg, I've been watching how hard you work around here. I think I could run the vacuum sweeper."*

*So, with superhero determination that was to characterize my dad for the rest of his life, the broken man relented, and a resolute man took his place. From that day on, Dad never complained or took a shortcut. He did whatever he had to do. When faced with a difficult job, he always tackled it first. Daddy earned respect from everyone whose path he crossed.*

*A five-year-old girl took it to heart. After all, how could her superhero be wrong?*

Jarred back to reality, an officer opened my door to pass me a dinner tray. I shrugged off the scared little girl that had watched black skin rolling off her daddy.

Later that evening, I recalled a recent conversation with Mom. She'd kept the darkest hours of Dad's recovery a mystery. Finally, she mustered the courage to share the truth, "Once, Dad woke up to see your grandma sitting at the foot of his bed with her rosary, and he said, 'Mom, if you're praying for me to live, just stop. I can't do this.'"

Had he given up on life, he'd have given up on us. On me.

*The pendulum of his life swung drastically from courage to despair and back again. Dad struggled mightily for months, the precipice of giving up and letting the burns win was the very same summit of triumph over which he claimed victory. Over time, and against all odds, Dad's spirit, and God's will, carried him back into the world and his body started to heal.*

*Months into the hospital stay, he reached a turning point, "Peg, I've decided that I'm going to make it through this. If I were to die, I know you would—and should—remarry. But I can't bear to have another man raise my children. I'm coming home."*

*Dad wouldn't be allowed to leave until he healed further, but his mind was made up. Many challenges lay ahead but none managed to be larger than his renewed spirit.*

*His scarred skin didn't flex like normal skin. Standing erect or walking while freely swinging his arms seemed an insurmountable feat. Dad pushed himself to heal, tearing into the task at hand, his children as his motivation. His determination drove him to prevail. After having nearly lost his war several times, love for us kids always brought him back.*

*Our family motto, which had previously been "let's go fly a kite," became "Phalens don't complain."*

*If Dad had the strength to not give up on life, shouldn't I find it also?*

I emerged the morning of the third day of suicide watch.

As if prison couldn't complete my breakdown, suicide watch took away all tangibles and intangibles, leaving me to start over. I found peace uninhibited.

God held the cards. There, somewhere in the sooty darkness of my wounded spirit, I felt a presence, almost as though all the fear and pain had delivered a glowing pearl of wisdom. Then, out from the shimmering halo around the pearl, a firefly of hope.

I feared what might be true if I opened my eyes but somehow

knew that it didn't matter, since either way, my eyes were open. I realized that I would live. With my eyes still tightly shut, I saw the harsh flickering fluorescent light above me change from nauseous yellow to blinding white. In awe, I wondered why the officer outside my door hadn't noticed.

Suddenly, for the first time since coming to suicide watch, I felt cozy, calm. I floated weightless in a warm pool; possibilities opened before me. My mother's face pushed into my mind. She loved me. Fiercely and unconditionally.

Then, I heard God speak. His voice rolled through me, calmly, assertively. I'd never heard it before although He sounded so familiar. My soul burned alive, and I knew it was Him.

"You will make it through this. And I'll be right here with you the entire way. You can do this and so much more. You were right to tell your story. This is just the beginning. Your story will change lives."

In a concrete cell, stripped of worldly distractions, the truth came to me. God loved me and nothing else mattered. Circumstances could never abscond with my peace. Only I could choose to take my eyes from God, and so I knew I must tell my story.

*I work, God gave me that gift, but I am a work in progress. I love my sisters and I've learned I may love a person without reciprocation. I cherish Mom's support and Dad's love, but God's love is the source of all.*

I no longer believed that I must be "Phalen Perfect" because Jesus said, "My grace is sufficient for you."

Dr. McCandless reveled in my new aura. "You seem resolved and happy."

"Now I understand the value of this suicide watch program. It works. I needed time alone to re-evaluate and de-stress. Thank you for seeing what I could not see."

Dr. McCandless smiled. Something in her eyes conveyed, for

a fraction of a second, some sense of self-satisfaction as though she took some credit, but before I could process the thought, her eyes shifted again to a message of gratitude and then to acknowledgement. Without a word, we knew something larger than us was at work. She turned her eyes to her paperwork to jot some notes.

I had grown beyond a hiding, frightened child. I chose a woman unashamed. My father's ghost whispered to me from the past. My spirit rose according to God's will to become the woman my world needed.

# 23.

## TWO BY TWO

**I ENTERED THE POD.** That Monday surfaced like any other, a bland indistinguishable element of weeks and months and years. What differed emanated from within me, a war-torn tigress with a destination.

Heads turned and a hush took the pod as I quickly made my way to my room where I found my bed had not yet cooled before prison staff assigned a new resident. The inmate that had taken my place immediately came to attention.

"Miss Toby don't worry. I'll put in a request to move. I'm glad you're back. Let me pack my things."

My roommates chimed in nervously, "All your stuff is here. We kept it safe for you."

If suicide watch taught me nothing else, it taught me humility. I held no grudge, my circumstances simply reconfirmed that I owned nothing here; I owned no time, nor space, not even a bed. However, that Monday offered a milestone, the beginning of a future which I would no longer take for granted.

Tuesday evening, U.S. Marshals took control. "Lockdown, ladies. Lockdown. There will be a transport tonight. Return to your cells. If you hear your name, pack your things. You'll be traveling to your designated federal prison. Take care of yourselves, ladies. We don't want to see you back here. Good luck."

"Young, Toby. Inmate 15186-031."

I had fifteen minutes to distribute my belongings to friends. Reggie handed me a slip of paper, "Here's my dad's address. I'd like to stay in touch."

"Thanks Reggie. Here's my mom's number. Call her tomorrow, let her know I'm gone, and that I'll call her as soon as I can, but it may be a few days. Tell her not to worry and that I love her."

Escape risks were highest during transports, so the entire facility locked down. Pod payphones were turned off so no one could inform outsiders about prisoner movements. Each inmate's destination remained sealed until just before departure.

With addresses inside the cover, my Bible provided some company. I smudged a bit of Vaseline inside my glasses case to serve as Chapstick. I hugged my roommates and stepped from my room into the pod, into a brave new future.

Four more months of my debt to society had passed since my return from TCF. I made a few new friends, but none took root as deeply as My Two Lisas. George had left the facility altogether and Lisa may well have since CCA isolated her from me and the rest of J-Pod. The announcement of my departure brought Lisa to the window in her door where she stood blowing kisses. With a heart symbol between her hands, she sent me off with as much love as she could offer.

For a moment, I closed my eyes and willed her confinement away, releasing Lisa to come wish me well on my journey, and I could wish her well on hers. I opened my eyes to our reality; she stood with her hand on the glass receiving my love. With her husband's contact info safely stored in my Bible, we would someday reconnect.

Officers led me to an unused area of the prison where beds

of concrete jutted out from the walls. As I walked into the room, Maria rushed to me with a fierce hug.

I excitedly greeted her, "Maria! *Mamacita!*"

With her typical Spanish accent, she mused, "Oh, Miss Toby. I'm so scared. Where are we going?"

"I don't know, but for now, we're together!" Too wound up to sleep, we talked and waited.

For the better part of two years, Mom had come nearly every week to support me, sometimes twice. I had not been strong enough to handle prison without her, but then, for the first time, my destination would likely take me beyond Mom's ability to visit. Awareness flashed over me. *My mom can't be here for the next segment of my incarceration. Wherever I'm going, I'll do it without her.*

Five, maybe six, hours passed, Maria and I, the only females traveling that day, still felt grateful to have each other. Just after four in the morning, an officer had us change into paper traveling outfits.

I noticed that Maria also wore long johns, as did I. I remarked, "It's freezing out there! We don't have coats. Can you imagine wearing these paper outfits without long johns?"

Shackled together, two by two, Maria and I entered the transport van, followed by a line of similarly shackled men, as if boarding Noah's Ark. Nervous, exhausted, and cold, my teeth chattered until the van warmed up. Two years, nearly to the day, had passed since the escape; with my head against the window, my mind sifted through the debris.

I couldn't believe it, I chuckled at that naive Toby who crumbled before at the thought of two weeks in jail. My final transition had begun after countless court appearances and six inter-prison transports. I couldn't recall what trivial source first informed me, but I knew that the first leg delivered all federal inmates to the Federal Transport Center (FTC) in Oklahoma City. From there, other transports would eventually deliver us to separate federal prisons throughout the country. I had surely been assigned a specific location, but for me, that cat remained in the bag.

Driving through the wintry night, we paused at a McDonald's in Wichita, Carly's hometown. In my mind, I called out a hello to her in Topeka, followed by a silent greeting, *Wichita, Carly says hi! She'll be here in a few years.*

Who knew, perhaps my future would allow me to visit.

An officer brought paper bags of steak, egg, and cheese bagels and orange sodas. Maria and I and ten male inmates cheered, ate, and then rolled the highways toward Oklahoma. At noonish, we arrived at FTC.

Shrouded in secrecy, FTC cultivated a spirit that encouraged federal inmates to create awesome urban legends to explain voids in the facts. Veterans of FTC proudly flaunted their experience as if surviving FTC compared to a medal of honor.

At the same time, we feared it. The federal prison system is managed by the Bureau of Prisons (BOP), a branch of the justice department. With approximately 157,000 inmates in more than 122 prisons, the FTC and ConAir were born of necessity. Built on a runway at the Oklahoma City airport, the FTC is a large dark brick building, all but invisible from civilization. Most inmates stay here for a week or two before taking a ConAir flight to a federal prison.

The prevailing boredom contrasted the amped-up officers that had arrested me. FTC officers spoke stoically, like listless cowboys ushering a herd through a feedlot.

At an elevator, Maria and I were directed to "Face the rear." Officers never allowed inmates to know their current location, much less their destination. Information endangered the staff more than any shank. The reality was, we'd just like to be a little less confused.

Facing backwards in an elevator easily ranked the list of

psychological triggers pulled by prison administrations throughout history. Tiny things stood monumentally to reduce my significance and attack my humanity, making me feel distant, maligned, and unworthy. Every movement, every finely tuned word, every pitfall of intentionally omitted information, spun my compass.

Maria and I hoped to be roommates when we got to our floor. The elevator hummed to a stop. One officer took Maria into one unit, the other took me to a second pod. I never saw Maria again, and I didn't even get to properly tell her goodbye.

The FTC pod shined with stunning sterility and a haunting silence. Nearly lifeless, FTC's inherent message echoed brevity. I made no comfort purchases, hobbled any tendency to grow roots, and maintained a vigilant posture against meaningful conversation.

A huge dayroom featured standard metal tables and stools bolted to the floor. Scrubby marks, peeling paint, graffiti, and blooms of black mold adorned other prisons, but not deep within federal lockup. FTC resembled a modern hospital operating room, only colder.

The feds issued khaki pants and shirts, the official prisoner's uniform. Luckily, they tolerated my long underwear.

My roommate, a girl from Kentucky who had embezzled from her job, shared nothing in common with me. Without books or other distractions, I chose to walk in the little joke that they called a yard. Five stories above the airport runways, the "yard" essentially differed from the dayroom because the exterior wall prevented me from enjoying any fulfilling view of the world. A wall of brick ten feet high, topped with a chain-link fence, offered a glimpse of sky and for a glorious twenty minutes each day, I could stand in a patch of sunlight. Overall, FTC earned no worthwhile memories, it merely provided a stopover while I waited for the last leg of my final transport, this time to a federal prison.

However, ConAir did not disappoint. The Justice Prisoner and Alien Transport System (JPATS) is an agency of the federal government charged with the transportation of persons in legal custody. It is the largest prison transport system in the world. The agency is managed by the United States Marshals Service out of the JPATS headquarters in Kansas City, Missouri. JPATS completes more than 260,000 prisoner movements per year.

I'm a convict that knows first-hand that ConAir is not movie fiction. My transport arrived in the form of an unmarked commercial jet.

"Smith 86472 Carswell, Fort Worth. Young 15186, Houston..."

"Aha! Finally, the big secret is revealed. Houston!" I waited with forty other women for processing. Like a well-oiled machine, U.S. Marshals strip-searched, handcuffed, and shackled us together in lines of three to accommodate triple-seated rows on the plane.

Worst of all, we all wore black boxes, torturous devices to cover the chains connecting the two handcuffs. Snapping them together made cuffs removable only by double unlocking. The box also held my wrists together at an unnatural angle.

Besides the forty or so women being transported, there were hundreds of men. Searching, shackling, and lining up this many inmates took several agonizing hours. Once locked into your chain gang, bathrooms were off limits. Together, we shuffled forward. The loading ramp, like any regular commercial airport, beckoned.

I wondered about John. He received an additional ten years for the escape, above and beyond the life sentence for murder and 118 months for grand theft auto. His debts reached beyond any human abilities.

*I doubt he'll ever be out. How is he coping with perpetual prison?*

*The paper reported that he'd been put into seg when he returned from the escape. Kevin told me that two years later he is still there. How does one cope with being in the hole more than two years straight?*

I winced a little from the pain in my wrist; an old riding injury made worse by the black box. ConAir had already proven itself uncomfortable.

Just before boarding the plane, an officer took a last cursory look at my Bible and glasses case. Pulling the case wide open, the officer barked, "What's this?"

"Vaseline for my chapped lips."

"You have three choices. Throw the case away, scrape it out, or turn yourself over to the FTC for time in seg. Sheepishly, I scooped the Vaseline out. My heart skipped a dozen beats at the thought of my own stupidity for risking it over chapped lips.

Heavily armed U.S. Marshals lined the loading ramp. Square-jawed intensity, tightly trimmed hair, Kevlar vests, earpieces, black boots, bold gold letters across their backs, assault weapons, and sunglasses, these men meant business. ConAir almost convinced me of the inherent threat to society posed by these plane-boarders... and me.

On an extra-large commercial jet, marshals occupied first class as ConAir integrated men and women with strictly enforced rules. I sat at the front of what might be called economy, with several empty rows behind first class before men filled the rear. While the male inmates took their seats, marshals scrutinized every twitch. Many male inmates would take any risk for a peek, touch, or smile. The tiniest of infractions would certainly escalate tensions to chaos.

Marshals also dispersed throughout the plane. They ordered the women, "Do not turn your heads. Make no eye contact."

The men were not ordered to keep their eyes from us. I guessed that the marshals reasoned those deprived male inmates wouldn't obey, so the onus rested with us women exclusively.

Meanwhile, my eyes absorbed the extra legroom granted me by virtue of front row privilege.

As soon as everyone was seated, marshals handed out a single apple and a six-ounce bottle of water. "This must last the entire day. And no bathroom access until arrival at your destination."

Not a fan of flying, I preferred road trips or trains, since takeoffs and landings sometimes made me queasy.

ConAir made a wide loop around the country to regular airports but never taxied to a gate. Instead, a remote runway with prison buses, vans, and police escorts awaited. As for the number of stops, I lost count, perhaps a dozen or more.

At each stop, the back belly of the plane dropped to the ground, and marshals, wearing sunglasses and wireless mics, spilled out to secure the tarmac. Forming a fully armed circle around the plane, they carried those same ominous black machine guns that had threatened me the night of my arrest. The scene both frightened and intrigued me.

Here, taxpayers' money funded a system with teeth, capable of handling the worst of the worst inmates in the world, organized crime leaders, and serial killers. If inmates aboard this plane were so extremely dangerous as to warrant this phenomenal show of force, how ironic was the benign presence of the Dog Lady of Lansing Prison?

Other inmates who had bused in were then corralled on the secured tarmac while select inmates deplaned ConAir to the buses. Transferring inmates would then board the plane for their trip back to FTC but not before ConAir had completed a full circuit around the country. At each stop, transfers required re-shackling and searching, since the hardware (handcuffs, shackles, and chains) remained as possessions of entities sending the inmates. Hundreds of inmates with tomes of paperwork had to be checked and re-checked. I seldom recognized the locale.

I dispensed tiny rations of my water, but by midday, it was gone. I wisely saved the apple until the end. Destination Houston neared the bottom of ConAir's daily itinerary. I learned to wait over the past two years, but this day was taxing my tolerance, and I hadn't peed for many hours.

I stood waiting on a Houston runway. ConAir had long since departed but getting everyone lined up outside the appropriate bus took forever; then, once loaded, buses took off in all directions, a movie-worthy scene.

My bus-mate, Mary, came from a state prison in Texas and, like me, had to finish out a federal sentence.

"Where you headed?" she asked.

"Houston, apparently."

Mary was neither Black nor White, nor Hispanic—sort of an olive complexion, like from Greece, Italy, or the Middle East—but Texan through and through. She tossed her thick black curly hair. On the smallish size, Mary seemed like she could handle the Texas heat.

"How about you?" I asked.

"This bus makes a stop in at the Houston Federal prison, but I'm going to Bryant."

She hadn't come by ConAir, instead, a bus brought her to the airport but stopped at Popeye's chicken for lunch. A crunchy chunk of chicken sounded awesome!

"Yeah, I've been waiting here for the last few hours. Even though it's February, the sun beating down on that tarmac is punishing."

Mary didn't look so good. I glanced at the officers in the front compartment, the air-conditioned space ahead of the glass partition. We were roasting back there in the closed compartment with the relentless sun streaming down on the full-sized un-opened windows.

*How can it be this hot in February?*

The day's stress, takeoffs and landings, those damned black boxes, no water. It was too much.

*How far away is Houston already?*

An unpleasant thirteen-hour day was made worse when Mary erupted like a power volcano of half-digested poultry. Shackled together, we avoided most of it. Two empty seats behind us seemed inviting, so Mary slipped around the end while I climbed over the seat back, trying to keep our chains from dragging through the vomit.

My wrists ached and the stench was overpowering. I was tired and thirsty and had to use the bathroom. I just wanted to go home. Closing my eyes, I pictured home—a little startled when the image that filled my mind were my women at CCA.

*Will I ever find another place that makes me feel as warm and loved as my women there had?*

Oblivious to the mess in the back of the bus, the officers, isolated in their air-conditioned pocket, joked and laughed. None of us bothered to tell them of Mary's regurgitated gift awaiting them. I survived the forty-five-minute drive into downtown Houston where my federal accommodations sort of resembled FTC, another high-rise indoor prison.

Unshackled in the holding area, a restroom offered my most immediate relief, and then I received a dinner tray. Once processed, the rear wall of an elevator took me to yet another indistinguishable gray concrete hallway. I entered the pod just before evening lockdown.

As foreboding as the prison images on the television show, an upper-tier ringed the open dayroom. Half-lit, the shadows of the empty room unnerved me. Even though this prison looked like Topeka and the FTC, the familiar layout did not disguise the ominous, aggressive spirits of this place. None of the other prisons had this effect on me. Somehow Federal Detention Center, Houston frightened me.

## 24

## ROMANCING THE THRONE

MANY PRISONS AND JAILS overtly occupy neighborhoods across our nation where innocent locals meander unaware. Urban high-rise prisons further refined the art of isolation. Where traditional prisons typically offered an outside yard with sunshine each day, Houston offered no such luxury. My tiny room felt more like being locked in a closet or a tomb.

From outside, windows in these facilities imply some sense of normalcy, yet their odd, tall, skinny slit shapes also hint at some medieval heritage like the architectural window designs of a castle. From inside, these apertures produce diluted daylight from opaque surfaces and reaffirmed my belief that civilization could no longer tolerate our presence.

However, of all the psychological tortures employed by the justice system, one of the most intolerable had relented for me. During many months of court proceedings, my yet-undefined future haunted me until an officer approached me in the pod. He held out an envelope and said, "Ms. Young?"

I tore it open while other inmates turned away from our card game to watch.

"I have a date! I have a date!" Like a schoolgirl invited to the prom, I stomped my feet in little circles and shook the envelope above my head. "April 30! That's my son's birthday, my lucky day, and the light at the end of my tunnel!"

Speaking of tunnels, high-rise prisons enabled a rather disgusting-yet-effective method of communication between inmates who took advantage of standard plumbing. By its very nature, plumbing connected all inmates. Evacuating water allowed sound to carry through the pipes to other cells. Inmates scooped out the water then pressed their faces tightly against the ring of the toilet, making a seal that forced sound to travel through the pipe. Answers back required a bit of shit-luck. It's called toilet talking. It was this very method of communication through which my old roommate Tee met her married-by-proxy husband who she was trying to divorce. But I had never seen it in action.

The administration strictly prohibited toilet talking which necessitated lookouts for the "poh-leese." I identified toilet talkers by characteristic, circular, pimply, oozing rashes. I intentionally avoided thinking much more about it.

In the room above ours, a woman discovered her true love by romancing the throne. Like children with cups on a taut string playing telephone, she sang Spanish lullabies nightly. A pillow over my head did little to muffle my crooning commode.

One day, our neighbor's lookout failed, and the pod officer caught our señorita singing. Her trip to the hole detoured when Señorita spotted her negligent lookout. She shoved a 300-pound officer off balance into a stainless-steel table and attacked her own accomplice, sending all of them across the polished concrete floor.

As all hell broke loose, more officers rushed in to assist. Blood, sweat, and tears, infused with Spanish profanity and mixed catcalls from throughout the pod, raised to a deafening crescendo. The two women pulled hair, scratched eyes, and slapped faces. Guards' demands went unheeded. Then, as quickly as it began, it ended.

Stressed by the event, officers called for lockdown immediately. With fewer than six months left on her time, the singing señorita got five more years for biting the officer. She didn't care. Her anger ebbed.

I pondered a woman's willingness to throw away life for a man she barely knew. At what point was the sacrifice worth the risk? I dismissed all similarities to my own situation. I knew John. I saw his face. Shared a friendship. Confided in the solace of a compassionate, insightful human being. We worked together, shared our stories. Shared our lives.

*Was she that desperate? Desperate… I know what that feels like. Lost and alone—I know that too.*

Perhaps from a different perspective, Señorita's story did mimic my own. It only took one act of desperation to spur the wheels of fate.

# 25.

## REDEMPTION ROAD

**AT A HEAVY COST,** our escape fed my inner wolf. Not only did I do time and shame my family and community, but I impugned my character. I betrayed myself when I betrayed the trust extended to me by the state of Kansas.

The burden stirred me to write to the warden of Lansing Correctional Facility. I apologized. I didn't expect a reply but received one immediately.

The warden wrote:

> Toby, I was pleasantly surprised to receive your letter. I appreciate your comments and kind words. I am also glad you found my interview to be reassuring. During that time (and since) I felt a lot of different emotions, but anger and resentment were not among them. Initially, it was fear for your safety—then more a sense of frustration and, to be completely honest, some feelings of betrayal. I do however still believe you to be a decent, kind, and caring person who made some bad decisions for reasons that are beyond my knowledge. I was glad to read that the last years and the system have been good for

you. I wish you well and every success and happiness as you move forward.

Dave

His letter encouraged me and filled me with wonder at the potential of human kindness.

*If Dave could forgive me, maybe I can forgive myself.*

\* \* \*

Tomorrow was my release day and my youngest son's birthday. Together, I viewed them as a good omen. Greg had not accepted my calls or answered my letters, but I believed we could mend things. Noisy thoughts kept me staring at the ceiling into the wee hours of the morning. Harassing me from a cobblestone slumber, anticipation swung randomly like a pendulum from a deep sense of trepidation to soaring hope. With a rather diminished sense of celebrity, my release inspired a few conversations sporadically throughout the morning. Women acknowledged me: some with a look, some with a thumbs up, some with a smile.

I had packed my box two days before and checked it many times. My release papers required my presence at the bus station at nearly half past one. As the morning dragged on, I had never felt more at the mercy of the prison administration. The arrival of lunch trays antagonized me more.

I confronted the pod officer, "I'm supposed to be released today. My bus leaves in an hour. What's going on?"

He dismissively answered, "They'll be here. Go sit down."

So I did, but the clock on the kitchen wall in my mind ushered in profound anxiety.

Tick.

Tick.

Tick.

Finally, an officer stepped into the pod. "Young, 15186?" I grabbed my box and release papers and unceremoniously followed the officer out of the pod, into the hallway to the elevator. I had done my time. Pre-conditioned, I faced the rear in silence. When the elevator floated to a stop, the door opened as I waited for a nudge, permission, or a command to leave. Instead, the officer simply said, "Let's go."

I turned uneasily. Something intangible had changed. The elevator rested at the first floor while the officer held the door. The officer's demeanor, not that he had softened, but I sensed some distant unidentifiable humanity. It felt like I had made it through the darkest part of a night and that, although the sun had not broken the horizon, the indications were implying that it would be there soon.

All the procedures, policies, and punishments utterly reprogrammed me to be submissive, an automaton which used exactly four sheets of toilet paper but only when instructed to do so. Twenty-seven long months of being told where and when to stand, sit, eat, and sleep ended unceremoniously as a corrections officer impatiently checked his watch.

I emerged like a timid puppy.

Before I went to prison, I envisioned our justice system as one that championed redemption and prepared inmates for reintegration, but I mistook its mission. No exit interview, no contemplation, and no advice from old friends prepared me for my release.

A corridor led to another room. My escort abandoned me, returning to the door from whence we came. I heard the door between us lock as he disappeared. For the first time in twenty-seven months, I was locked out rather than in.

A female officer facilitated a change out of my drab khaki uniform. "Your mom sent this," she said, handing me a package. I eagerly pulled out my clothes, I recognized them and held them in wonder, caressing the shirt against my face. The clothes were mine, but I wasn't me. Forty pounds heavier and shorter on confidence, I couldn't possibly squeeze in them, so I took the prison-issued, complimentary blue jeans.

The officers' behavior, the lock, my clothes, and then something else unusual struck me. There, in a corner: a curtain, a makeshift dressing room, a hint of human dignity! Oppression dominated every prison inch of this side of that curtain; freedom hovered beyond. As a free woman my crevices no longer required investigative scrutiny at every turn.

Dark blue and dorky, the jeans fit. The shirt Mom sent was too small, but the officer urged me to wear it anyway. I simply couldn't muster the resistance so I writhed in with determined force as it resisted the invasion; I hoped the seams would cooperate.

I signed more papers. The officer handed me cash, "gate money" they called it, for incidentals and transportation expenses. Leading me to the visitors' check-in counter, two more officers dissected me and my paperwork one last time.

Federal prison never awarded me the light of day. A window in a door at the other end of this room glowed with my future, or maybe just sunshine. "Okay, Ms. Young. You're all set. Go out that door and catch a cab to the bus station. Your bus leaves at one twenty-five. If you're not on it, we'll know, and you'll be in violation of your parole."

I found myself on a sidewalk in Houston with a head full of worries and a box full of books—neither of which helped me with bus stations, taxis, the time, nor how to begin anew with felony convictions. I possessed a cardboard box the last time I left prison, except that one concealed a convict.

A bit dizzied, more worldly, and wiser from the prison experience, I had completed the circle; I was free.

The U. S. Government required my presence at the bus

station, but I had no idea how to get there. Told to get a cab and without a watch, imaginary seconds ticked in my head like the clock on the kitchen wall during the weeping willow tragedy. Traffic, car horns, bustling people, and ungodly heat rattled me. My box grew heavier by the second and my shirt felt tighter. I couldn't just stand there hoping for a taxi that might never arrive while my bus rolled away on the other side of town. Shifting my box to the other hip, I climbed back up the steps and went in the door from which I left.

The officers immediately intercepted. "What are you doing? You can't come in here. You need to leave."

"Where's the bus station? Can I walk?"

"No, you can't walk—it's five miles away!"

"Well, how am I supposed to get there?"

"Just wait outside on the sidewalk for a taxi to come."

"I've never flagged a taxi before. How do you do it? Exactly where should I stand?"

Shooing me out the door with their hands flapping, they gave a final word of advice, "Wait."

Back on the sidewalk, I set my box on the ground. A taxi drifted up beside me. The cabbie knew the look, bright blue unwashed jeans, and a cardboard box.

"Need a ride to the bus station?"

I settled in for a ride in the cool air-conditioned car. Then it hit me. The officers took pleasure in this one last jibe, one last disparagement. They knew the Houston streets were foreign to me. They denied me any sense of time yet stressed its urgency and the consequences I'd suffer. They intentionally placed me on the street without the tiniest bit of information that might help me cope. And if that weren't enough, they added remarks that generated a sense of helplessness and fear. They called this cab but used the event to further assault my confidence.

*How precarious is my freedom? Will everyone I encounter set me up to fail? Is this just another part of the system I will need to learn to navigate? I thought parole would be an easy no-brainer. But, what if it's not?*

Ten minutes later I was at the bus station.

"Here we are. You just go inside, and they'll have your ticket at the counter. Have a good life and enjoy your freedom." The warm, caring attitude of the cabbie refreshed me.

Dozens of buses lined up outside the huge bus terminal. My appetite flared at the sight of McDonald's just inside the door. Without lunch, fries and a coke sounded blissful. "Welcome to Greyhound. Where are you traveling today?"

"Kansas City"

"Great, you'll be at Gate 14. Do you have your ticket?"

"I was told it would be at the counter."

"Who purchased the ticket for you?"

"The BOP."

"Ohhhh." Her tone immediately turned frosty. "ID?"

I slid my prison ID across the counter. With that damned box of books in my arms and a bus ticket in my teeth, I passed by McDonald's; I didn't deserve, nor did I have time, to eat.

*Did they have to wait til the last possible minute to release me? What would have been wrong with an extra twenty minutes?*

I barely made it as I took a window seat near the front of the bus. A small man in a Greyhound uniform greeted me with a laugh, "Hey there, Missy—how's your day?" His southern accent tickled my ears, his spirit infected me and made me smile.

"It's good. It's been a long time coming. It's a good day."

My box found a home on the rack above me, and I settled in. I hadn't been released for an hour yet, and I felt the tug of war between hope and shame.

*It is different out here.*

Confidence would be harder to maintain.

The bus driver watched for a moment, the creases in his smile cartwheeled across his face into a frown and all the way back to the same delightful smile. "Well," he said, tipping his hat back to scratch his head, "I think it's time." He closed the door, took his seat, and looked at the oversized mirrors as the bus lumbered out. "Yes, ma'am, it's time to go."

Tales of sleepy bus stories trailed off to the back seat of my mind. I stared out the window at the city lights and a different future. We stopped every ten minutes at some little corner that served as a bus station. It had been an hour and we still weren't out of the city limits. It was going to be a *long* fifteen-hour bus ride to Kansas City.

To me, twenty-seven months in prison seemed like eons. Not only had time passed without me, but the world had changed. Before the escape, I topped an American pedestal. As a felon, riding a bus back to Kansas City, I began to understand that the world not only expected me to fail, but it had raised the bar of success to nearly unachievable heights.

Our communities accept and protect disadvantaged people. Emotionally, physically, and mentally challenged people receive opportunities to independently flourish. Felons, most of whom suffer from a lack of character, education, and natural talent are provided no rehabilitation nor any viable second chances. Worse yet, most don't care.

*In some ways, the escape seems like only yesterday. The draining whirlpool of constant emotional battles exhausted and overwhelmed me; I barely functioned. I couldn't sleep. I couldn't eat. I couldn't go on. And I couldn't stay in the life I loathed.*

*That morning, I expected a farm wagon at the gate. My pulse outraced my frantic thoughts. Fear and confusion stood in the shadows of love and hope.*

*Officers stared with expectation. Monotonous daily transactions at this guard station conditioned them to expect a certain behavior. With my impeccable rapport, the guards suspected nothing. I, on the other hand, expected wailing tones rising and falling like a rotating tornado siren, jerking everyone within five miles awake to this insane plan. The most subtle twitch of doubt—an eyebrow raised, pupils flared, breath too shallow, or the slightest creak, crack, or wiggle in my voice, any tiny thing—could set sirens wailing.*

*Hundreds of dress rehearsals I had innocently drilled every day for months coming and going with prison dogs, getting to know the routine and the guards and weaknesses of the system; I knew exactly how to behave. The fact was, no other person on the planet could have pulled this off. Nobody. Not even other volunteers transitioned these gates like I did.*

*I pictured John's grinning hazel eyes and his easy-going stride. I took the lead, but John directed the show. Submission felt foreign, exciting. My heart pounded for John and in mere moments, we would be together.*

*Am I really doing this? Are we doing this?*

*I deliberately stepped from the warm security of the shack, into the unforgiving cold. I felt myself shiver. Was it nerves? Or the temperature? Opening the back doors of the van, I gestured to the handlers. "Load 'em up."*

*Guards watched. Time stood still. What if our own dogs smelled the crate, or a guard heard a sneeze or a cough? Perhaps the van wouldn't start, or the officer uncharacteristically decided to search the van. My mind raced with all the things that could go wrong; any of which would be a game stopper. A convicted murderer in my van could not be explained away to prison staff.*

The bus eased to a stop and the change in momentum woke me up. We were stopped in Oklahoma City for an hour layover. I bought a T-shirt that fit and some dinner.

In the ladies' room, I flipped on the light to a scattering of roaches with the faces of my sisters and sons and ex-husband and reporters and strangers who pointed and stared. They scurried down drains and into cracks and above ceiling tiles to avoid me, to avoid the light. The truth was that I wasn't perfect, they weren't perfect, my marriage wasn't perfect, and my escape was far from perfect.

The late hour lent itself more to sleeping than watching my new free world outside of the bus window. Yet I couldn't close my eyes to the life which passed as Kansas City approached. We had never been more divided—Kansas City and me.

Pulling into the KC terminal at seven o'clock in the morning, my heart raced at the familiar sights. My box and I were once again on the sidewalk looking for a cab. This time it was easier. The cabbies were practically pulling people into their cabs.

"Can you take me to Leavenworth?" I asked as one pulled up.

"Baby, I can take you wherever you wanna go." I could tell he loved to talk. "Where are you going in Leavenworth?"

"I don't know the address, but I can direct you to it."

"Is it a business?"

"Yes. I guess you'd call it that."

"Well, I probably know where it is then. What's the name?"

"It's a halfway house."

"Oh, you work there."

I figured now was the time to start addressing my past, so I answered boldly, "No, I don't work there. I'm going to be a resident. I was just released from federal prison in Houston, Texas." Hurriedly, I added, "I'm not really a bad person. I'm not going to rob you or anything."

"Honey, I knowed all kinna folk who been to prison. I ain't scared of you. Not one little bit." Laughter filled the cab. "Ain't that sumthin'."

I smiled back.

# 26.

## THE JAGGED EDGES

INMATES NEARING THE END of sentences often didn't see the proverbial end of their rope. Most spent months flailing at halfway houses while flaccid administrations scrutinized every turn, hawkishly searching for any sign of justifiable behavior to send the inmate back to prison. Penitentiaries never provided encouragement, programs, job-skills training or support of any kind; they simply expected inmates to miraculously deal with the pressures of old habits, job searches, and independence.

With only two months left on my sentence, the feds were compelled to shorten my stay at the halfway house to a mere three weeks. With my halfway house crushed against the boundary fence of CCA, the physical proximity reminded me how precarious my liberties had become.

The lobby resembled that of an average hotel except the clerk behind the window offered breathalyzers rather than a room key. The spacious lobby belied the constrictions of the ensuing concrete hallway. On the left, the kitchen contrived nasty meals for the Leavenworth County Jail where its legendary reputation preceded its menu. During my stay there, I had heard of this kitchen across town; seeing it first-hand did nothing more to whet my appetite.

Adjacent to the kitchen a door opened into the women's dorm where metal bunks were placed along half-walls, giving some remote semblance of privacy. At the rear a large bathroom offered multiple toilet stalls, curtained showers, and something I hadn't seen in a long time—mirrors! Real mirrors, with glass.

I had just arrived. Sleep had come sporadically in short, unrestful naps on the bus, but the sunshine and excitement of the first day of the rest of my life had never been more energizing. I waited anxiously.

Three months passed since I'd seen Mom and eight months since we touched. When I saw her walk down that sidewalk, I ran straight into her arms. Both of us laughed and cried and held each other for longer moments than we thought possible.

"You made it Toby. I'm so proud of you. I always knew you could. You're stronger than you know."

"There were times I didn't think I would, Mom."

I looked over her shoulder at CCA. "Crazy to think I spent fifteen months there. It looks just as ugly from this side of the fence. There's the women's yard Mom," I said, pointing across the grass. "That's where we got to go outside."

I got quiet. Mom said, "You know, don't you?"

"Yeah, it was on the news in Houston. Lisa's been sentenced to death."

I looked into Mom's eyes, she knew Lisa and Lisa's family from visits in those buildings behind the chain-link fences, but Mom's eyes told me that she cared about me, "Maybe you can write to her."

"I can't, Mom. I know it's stupid but if I'm on paper I can't have any contact with another felon. Makes no sense at all. Who else can relate to me?"

"You won't be on probation forever Toby."

"No, but Lisa needs me now, not in two or three years."

Mom squeezed my hand. "Let's go get some lunch and some

clothes."

Mom watched me staring at people walking by. She watched while I drank in sights, sounds, and smells. She watched as I picked up my fork and slid it under real food and relished the moment. She watched as I absorbed the lost world around me, and for a moment, I remembered John's short dream of a life beyond the bars and the cinder blocks.

The heavenly food dazzled my tongue; I couldn't help but close my eyes and imagine the starry skies above my bus that brought me home the night before. Did anyone realize how absolutely stunningly beautiful it is? *How beautiful is life and our world?*

Walmart overwhelmed me. So many things and so many people. I didn't know where to look, or what to do. Part of me wanted to run back to the parking lot and hide in the car, but Mom took my hand and we bought pajamas and the softest maroon slippers with a big fuzzy bow, jeans and T-shirts, underwear, and a bra. A bra! A real bra. In prison we had one size fits all sports bras that we wore twenty-four hours a day.

Best of all, Mom guided me to the book aisle where I picked out several books to take back with me. "I should probably get a library card, Mom."

"And a driver's license. We'll do that tomorrow. Your brother bought a new car. He's gonna let you drive his old one till you make some decisions. Oh, Toby, I'm so happy you're home. My heart is about to burst." Mom's contemplative wrinkles around her eyes popped as a distant thought took her attention. "Oh, Toby, I almost forgot." She produced a cell phone from her pocket, "Alden sent this for you." I took it, a new symbol of my future, pondering for a moment what this meant.

I looked back at her, "Thanks, Mom."

Compared to my time behind bars, my first day with Mom freshened me, decorating my heart with flowers and colors and crystal-clear waters—feelings of a new beginning. But the day waned, and the sun grew tired at the horizon as we stood at the front door to the halfway house.

Mom sighed, squared her shoulders to me, and said, "Toby, there's something else… Greg is in the hospital. He has cancer. Maybe we'll know more tomorrow." Like the day that Dad was burned, Mom's eyes reminded me that we would find our way through this too.

I hugged her once more, held back my tears and said, "Stay strong, Mom."

In an instant, countless bits of emotion spiraled around me. Like the curved legs of a galaxy, each important topic in my life: my family, John Manard, my career, my felony, even the drama of my release on that very day, suddenly blinked out of existence, taken by one single event. Greg's life hung at the edge and nothing else mattered.

*Cancer! How can that be? Will God really take two of my children? Dad told me that wouldn't happen. God wouldn't do that. Oh, my poor boy. All alone. Who will be there for him? Can it be me? Will I be allowed? Oh, my poor, poor boy.*

Stunned by the news, I sorted my new Walmart things, settled on my bed, and tried to call Eric. Surely Eric knew more. Everyone knew I'd be home that day; Eric and I had spoken on the phone a few days before. He had agreed to meet me for dinner in the next few weeks.

No answer.

I thought, *That's strange.* I tried again. No answer.

I looked more closely at my new cellphone unsure of its reliability. Smartphones hadn't been developed before I went away, but I knew I could figure it out. I poked around its programs enough to reveal messages; there were none.

The need in me for connection grew, my mind queried, *How odd.* Eric said I could call him. I left my new phone number, yet again, in another message and waited. My mind raced with reasons, none so disappointing as the truth.

The next day, I waited on the picnic table in the morning sunshine. Mom and I had plans for day two. The driver's license bureau and perhaps some initial job searches; although Boston pulled me easterly, conditions for my release required immediate employment, the greatest hurdle for most recently released inmates. So, with more questions than answers, and Greg's prognosis weighing on me, I turned to urgent requirements.

Warm bright sunshine on my face and cool green grass between my fingers reminded me to breathe and appreciate and love. *Sweet!*

More joyful than Mom's previous arrival, we struck the day with verve. However, once settled in the car, I sensed something askew.

Mom said, "Your sister went to the hospital yesterday. She told Rob you had been released. He had no idea. She thought he might pass out when he heard the news. His first question: 'Where is she? She's not coming here, right?'"

Mom continued her story, "Eric spoke up and said, 'She's in a halfway house in Leavenworth.' Rob then turned on Eric, 'Oh, I see now. You've been talking to her, haven't you? I should have known you couldn't hold out. You don't have the courage not to talk to her. You don't have the courage to give her what she deserves.' Rob was disgusted; he said, 'I'm not a bit surprised. I should have known.'"

*Eric faced an unsavory choice; nobody should have to choose one parent over the other. But life unfairly fills the world with difficulties. I, too, would have to prioritize relationships, time, and purpose.*

I stared out the window as poles, trees, and mailboxes drifted before my eyes. My heart ached to comfort Greg. I asked, "How did he get sick, Mom? What kind of cancer is it?"

"Hodgkin's Lymphoma. He hasn't felt good for months.

Thought he had the flu, but never got any better. Finally, Rob told him to go to the emergency room. Greg drove himself there and they drew some blood and sent him home. Before he even got to the driveway, the hospital called him and told him to come back but not to come alone, bring someone with him."

"What's the plan?"

"He'll start chemo. Here's the hard part for you, Toby. After Rob's tirade, Greg requested that you not be welcomed. He looked at Rob and said, 'I don't want to see her.'"

I eyed the world rushing past as my heart shattered. No words came.

Mom wasn't done, "Rob blames you for Greg's cancer. He says if you'd been home where you belonged, you would have taken him to the hospital sooner, and it never would have gotten this far."

Angry at Rob and with life, I opened my mouth and let my feelings fall out, "How could Rob not see how his own words implicate him? We are Greg's parents; why couldn't Rob be bothered enough to notice?" I continued for long minutes in silence while my mind wandered and Mom drove. Then more words came out, "Greg is not a kid anymore; at twenty-four years old he had a duty to manage his own health. Why didn't he get help?" More thoughts and feelings circled in me until I voiced them too, "Perhaps, had I been there for Greg, I would have made a difference."

Mom grabbed my hand, "I don't understand how this is happening Toby. I am so disappointed in Rob, and I'm so sorry I didn't see it sooner and tell you to leave your marriage. We'll get through this." She squeezed tightly and then said, "Now that we've got all this mess out in the open, let's try to enjoy our day. I'm so glad you're home."

My driver's license was easy—it hadn't expired yet, so they were able to just print me a new one on the spot. After lunch, we stopped at a department store so I could see about a job. The manager was thrilled with my skills and work history. Practically drooling to get me started, he asked, "Do you have a preferred schedule?"

"No, I can basically work any shift you need me."

"Would you be interested in managing a department? Or, better yet, the nighttime stockers?"

"Sure. That would be fine. Either one."

"When can you st—" His voice trailed off and his face tightened. I knew he'd just seen the checked box. That nasty little box on job applications that says, "Check if you are a felon."

"Actually, we don't have openings right now. Thanks for coming in." He could barely wait for me to make it all the way through the door before he firmly shut it behind me.

Freedom didn't feel so free.

I had similar experiences everywhere else I tried. Nobody wanted to hire a felon. I really couldn't blame them.

One of the girls in the halfway house had a job at a chair manufacturer. "Toby, my boss is looking for someone to run the office. If you're interested, I'll tell him about you."

I got that job and I loved it. Every employee in his shop was a felon. It's a good way to get a lot of help for lower wages. Add to that the $2,500 tax credit for hiring a felon and it suddenly becomes fiscally responsible. All his employees were either currently living at the halfway house or had been there and continued working after they were released.

The office was a mess, and I dove into organizing it. My ability to manage complex tasks impressed my boss who never before employed a college-educated worker. He knew about my Boston job offer and courted me to stay in Kansas City and take on more responsibility in the office.

Alden and I were still talking about his job offer, but parole offices move slowly. Very slowly. I wasn't pushing too hard because I enjoyed being with Mom. And now, with Greg's cancer, maybe I should stick around. I had a job I liked and a place to live.

After three short weeks in the halfway house, I moved in with Mom. She loved having me around.

"Toby, you are such a delight to be with. You make my days brighter. I've been watching you. You walk outside and just smile. You look around and fall in love with things none of us even notice. You make me see the world in a totally different light and it is beautiful, isn't it?"

The one thing that wasn't so beautiful was the absence of my sisters. They'd been stopping at Mom's regularly, but now that I'd moved in, they were busy with other things. I knew Mom felt bad about it. Eric had stopped taking her calls too. I was a pariah, making Mom's life harder than it should be. People pointed at me in restaurants and shopping centers. Alden's proposal shone in a new light.

*It would be nice to go somewhere where nobody knew my name.*

One morning a friend from the halfway house called me. "Toby, you need to come and get this dog. He's just a tiny little thing and he's running around on the highway. He's going to get killed. And he stinks. Oh, does he stink! I don't know where he's been, but he needs help."

I groaned.

*I don't want to be back in the dog rescue business. I promised Mom I wouldn't bring a dog home. But he obviously needs help. It wouldn't hurt to just go see what's going on...*

I told my boss, "I'm going on a short errand. I'll be right back."

"Sure thing."

I returned with an eight-week-old schnauzer poodle mix puppy crawling with fleas, covered in sludge, stinking to high heaven, and just as happy as could be.

"You aren't keeping him in here, are you?"

"Not for long. I have a plan."

Ms. Johnston, my savior officer at CCA had a dog grooming business in town. We talked about it often and I remembered the business name.

"Of course, we'll work him in Toby. It'll be good to see you on this side of the fence," she said when I called her.

At the end of the day, I left with an adorable, little, red-bowed, black and white, curly haired puppy, and a part time Saturday job bathing dogs at the grooming shop.

I dreaded bringing a new dog home. Mom had made clear her one directive. "Now, don't be bringing any new dogs around Toby. We have two already you can play with."

There I was, with the best of intentions, still dragging home another stray.

"Mom, a friend of mine from the halfway house called about this little guy. He was a mess and needed help. Look how cute he is! He'll be easy to find a home for."

Throughout the evening, Mom watched us together, until she surprised me, "I think you should name him Checkers. It might be good for you to have a pet."

Rubbing his ears, I agreed, "Welcome home, Checkers!" A giant grin stretched across my face. With a furious wag of his tail, flashes in his coal-black eyes, and a high-pitched yip, Checkers sealed the deal.

# 27.

## BOSTON BECKONS

**I LEFT PRISON, BUT JOHN** proved a harder habit to break. I read every one of his letters each night before I fell asleep. Deep down, I knew I couldn't live the rest of my life crying over a stack of letters that bound me to him. Moving on challenged me, but I knew I had to rebuild a life for myself without him.

"Tom, can you build a fire for me?" I asked my brother in a moment of strength.

"Sure thing, Toby. Would Dad's burn barrel do?"

"Perfect," I said, grateful to have a man around who cared about me the same way Mom did.

*Of course, Dad's burn barrel! What better place to get rid of the ties that bind?*

Truth be told, the escape on February 12, 2006, followed a multitude of transgressions. I erred when, at five years old, I assumed unassigned duties. I failed when, as a teenager, I did not confront my dad about coping with his tragic accident and instead dove into clubs and school activities. I wrote off a more meaningful relationship with Rob when I didn't push for a stupid game of golf or *at least* respect.

After twenty-eight years of abject obedience, I compromised my principles when John Manard sashayed into my world. When

John stood close to me in the privacy of the band room at the prison, my breath gave me away, and John took what I couldn't refuse. Take your pick. Perhaps, had I had the power to control my unleashed spirit, I could have foregone the convictions.

"Stay with me, Tom. I need a witness." Holding them up, I said, "These are letters, songs, and poems from John Manard. Newspaper articles about him." Tears streamed down my cheeks as I fed the fire. I burned each letter and burned the bridge, then I remembered one more thing.

After Rob and I wed, I had cleaned and packed my dress in layers of tissue paper, in the hopes that one day my daughter might wear it. It was one of the items Rob so bitterly tossed from his truck. I carried this box to Dad's burn barrel and fed my beautiful lace dress into the fire. It burned with a putrid smell and greasy black smoke.

I began to love me and prayed that somewhere, someone might love me without conditions.

Tougher than I thought, being home challenged me. I lost my sons. I could no longer navigate my sisters. Dad's passing and my scandal ended our family unity. Christmas gatherings, casual phone calls to family, lunches at the Plaza with my sisters, all faded.

Alone, I occupied the moral low ground. I regretted creating circumstances that all but forced Mom to choose between us. Perhaps I could heal far from the notoriety and broken family dynamics. Perhaps Greg's chemo would go smoothly and when he healed his affliction, he'd be more open to healing us. Perhaps we all needed space, time to find ourselves, and fresh starts. Perhaps the time had arrived for me to go.

Alden offered us a trip to Boston to meet him, view the offices, and learn more about his project before I decided. He also threw in a year's pre-paid lease on a condo in his building. I informed him, "I have a dog."

Alden answered, "Not a problem. You can even bring him to work with you. It will be nice to have a dog in the office."

My parole officers, who had been dragging their feet, thought a trip to Boston might reveal a disappointment or confirm our hopes—either way, a good idea.

"Here's your travel papers. You probably won't need them but keep them with you at all times. And call us when you've seen enough to decide," they told me.

Mom and I flew to Boston. Alden picked us up at the airport and took us to a restaurant on the shore. We took seats on a large deck over the water. The bright sun mirrored across the bay. Seagulls squawked nearby, as the waves hushed against the vast beach; Mom inhaled deeply the fresh, salty air and smiled at me.

Kansas City troubles seemed to drift away on the tides. Alden knew to use the features Boston had to offer, and he took the time to honor my mom with polite descriptions of the old city.

"Toby will love it here. We have some of the top schools and hospitals in the world. Boston sports are world-class. We have deep, rich American history, with the Plymouth Colony, Plymouth Rock, and Salem, where the witch trials convened. We have museums and the New England Aquarium to explore." Alden held a cold cranberry vodka and swept his arm in a wide gesture to the sea, "And then we have the Atlantic!"

We later returned to the airport where he rented a car and handed me the keys. He said, "Enjoy Boston. Here's the address for your hotel, and the address for the office. I'll show you around in the morning."

The next day, we made our way to the office about ten minutes north of Logan Airport and twenty minutes from downtown Boston. Alden's office was in the center of Lynn, built in the late 1800s as a commercial property for the gas and electric company, and it had taken on a new purpose as condos. Street side spaces continued in a commercial capacity while Alden maintained a business and home in the basement. The second and third floors featured gorgeous residences—most privately owned.

While Mom cuddled Alden's new baby, we also met a guy named Chris, Alden's right hand; they had grown up together in the rugged Downeast Coast of Maine. Alden remained rather inconspicuous while Chris filled the room. With a blond crewcut and work boots, Chris feared nothing and gave his heart to hard work and dirty hands.

Sitting in our hotel room, Mom and I analyzed our weekend over a game of cards that I'd learned in prison. She beat me, three games in a row!

Mom asked, "What did you like best, Toby, about everything we saw this weekend?"

"I would love living in the middle of so much history. And I love the idea of taking the train everywhere I need to go."

Mom looked out the window and said, "I think it's lovely to be able to smell the sea. I like a small organization with just you and Alden and Chris. I really like Chris; he seems like someone you could get to know."

I shared Mom's stare out the window, "I like that nobody here knows my story."

"Okay, plenty to love. What concerns you?"

"Only that you're so far away. And Greg—what if he needs me?"

"It's a short plane ride home, Toby. I'm sure Chris would watch Checkers. Also, I'll come back to Boston to visit. I'd love to explore more: Salem and Cape Cod. I'll definitely return now that I have a place to stay!"

Having decided, we gave the move four thumbs up. I called my parole officers on the way to the airport. "I think this will be a good place for me to start over."

My federal parole officer asked, "What does your mother

think?"

"She agrees. It was a good weekend. Alden seems like a decent guy. I met Chris, whom I'll be working with. Seems like it will just be the three of us. Oh yeah, and my dog is no problem."

"Okay, I'll get the paperwork started. You'll be transferred to a federal parole officer in Massachusetts, but I'll still be the owner of your case. You can call me anytime if you need advice or help. I really hope this works out for you, Toby. Give your mom my best."

My federal parole officer had dropped by Mom's several times before I was released from prison. They bonded over tea and my parole officer learned she could trust Mom's judgment. With Mom's blessing, the parole offices quickly completed the paperwork and authorized my move.

Rob wouldn't allow me on the property, so my brothers drove the rented U-Haul to my old home. They loaded items granted in the divorce. Not only had I no opportunity to walk the property or see a comprehensive inventory of our stuff before the divorce and had to make requests from memory, but even the day that my brothers retrieved my stuff, I had no idea what made it into the truck *or didn't.*

In our divorce, Rob agreed to pay me for some equity in our house. For twenty-eight years I'd earned two-thirds of our income, but I simply needed to be done. Rob owed me more— much more—but I wanted to make it on my own. I knew it would be a hard-scrabble journey to start over at fifty-one with no job and a felony conviction, but I'd learned nothing good came easy and challenges inspired me.

With a not-so-subtle contempt threat my attorney nudged Rob to pay me, which he did by check in my mother's mailbox, the day before I left for Boston.

With U-Haul windows down, puppy in my lap, money in the bank, sister-in-law next to me, and my brother behind the wheel,

I left the Midwest for sunrises over the ocean.

We made stops along the way. At Lake Erie, Tom and I skipped rocks like when we were kids while Checkers tried to retrieve them. I filled a bag with shell fragments.

"Toby, leave the shells. We're crowded enough with three people and a dog in the cab of the truck!" Susie squeezed into the middle bench for most of the twelve hundred miles. I tried it once only long enough to appreciate Susie's sacrifice.

One day from Boston, Niagara Falls presented an opportunity.

I pleaded, "Tom let's stop! One more night on the road but the falls will be worth it!"

And they were. Watching all that cascading water made me feel tiny. The fine mist drifted over me, and I thought, *Anything is possible.*

We arrived in Boston after dark. Alden met me with the keys and called Chris to help us unload the truck.

My top-floor loft apartment was darling. I could see the ocean from my window.

*A place of my own! My very own. I could fit ten of my prison cells in this apartment that most people might consider small. So much space and it's just me. I have never had anything that was all mine. I love this! I can do whatever I want, whenever I want. I can decorate and feel at home. I won't have to be busy with projects. I can just stay home and learn to relax.*

*Oh! These windows—velvet. I need to find velvet drapes. Purple, I think. I see my home as purple—olive green. Yes, that will be perfect. I could put the bed there in front of the windows. Or I could put my desk there and move the bed over here. Or maybe just put the bed next to the door and let all this open space be where I work and read and relax...*

Called out of my ponderings, Alden asked, "Where should I put this mattress?"

"Just lean it against the wall here by the door, I'll figure it out later."

I hurried down to the truck to see how I could help. Chris and Tom helped move furniture out and up the elevator. The few things I brought from Mom's had been unloaded, and I began to see items from Rob. Dirt and dust covered everything.

Tom said, "This stuff came from the barn where it had been stored for three years."

Had I known, I'd have left most of it behind. I spent the next few days cleaning furniture and unpacking boxes while Tom and Susie went off and explored Boston. I went with them a couple of times, but I had a new life to build, and I itched to get started. My dream began to breathe.

I put the bed next to the front door, which seemed odd, but it worked. I felt the rest of the space wanting to be open. The first big room emerged as my bedroom, office, living room, and library. Olive green velvet curtains caressed the exposed brick.

The second room featured a generous eat-in kitchen, which I made a sitting room with a small loveseat, an outdoor wrought iron glass-topped table and two chairs from a local thrift store. At the end of the L-shaped space, a walk-in closet below a loft coaxed me to fill it with shoes, bags, and belts. I slept up in the loft a couple of nights, but the ladder proved impossible for Checkers, so I preferred the bed in the main room. The huge bathroom accommodated my own washer and dryer.

Tom and his wife settled me in, toured a little of Boston, and flew home to Kansas City a week later, leaving me with finishing touches and my first steps into a new job and life.

With maybe a dozen other condos on my floor, I had the first apartment at the very end of the hallway. The elevator and stairway were right next to my apartment. To go to the basement for work, Alden provided a special key to the elevator which granted me access.

Checkers and I learned that the elevator doors opened facing west when we went to the basement. Any other time, they opened facing east.

Checkers sat quietly in the elevator, usually with a ball in his mouth. He knew if the door opened front, he was going for a walk and playing fetch in the park. If the door opened rear, Checkers would dash from the elevator, down the ramp, dropping a toy at Chris's feet, his tail wagging furiously.

Checkers fell in love with Chris. Chris fell for Checkers. I took my time.

## 28

## THE HINGE SQUEAKS

**THE MAYFLOWER IN PLYMOUTH** belonged to the pilgrims. Historically, the ship represented oppressed people who searched for religious freedom in a new land, yet Salem's witch trials proved that nobody escapes intolerance. Then, the ride of Paul Revere, "The redcoats are coming, the redcoats are coming," expressed how desperate people were to shrug off their British marriage.

Sounded perfect to me, like I'd come to the right place.

Mom kept me abreast of Greg's battle; we hoped for the best. Boston's distractions helped but didn't entirely curb my pain. At high tide, the Atlantic kissed the retaining wall along the road where Checkers and I would take long walks between stints of work. The tide's extraordinary retreat revealed a sandy beach at the base of the wall and dark mud beyond, accessible by a long set of concrete stairs.

I explored my new city through heavy traffic, partially caused by ancient trails which had gradually evolved into city streets. Natural boundaries of stone, hills, trees, and waterways had originally dictated the direction of travel, but with a city built between the streets, the modern result resembled chaos. Several centuries of development encouraged both prosperity and gridlock.

The elevator provided a vertical commute, an express lane bypassing all traffic. I began to wrap my head around the work and the daily routine, processing the goals that Alden set for us. I spent most hours working in the office.

Chris and Alden bounced between technical applications, business endeavors, manual labor, and travel. One afternoon, I caught a conversation between them about a laborer who had worked for them for many years but was recently locked up in a jail in Portland, Maine.

Chris said, "I should probably write to Oscar and see what it's going to take to get him out of there."

I chimed in, "Do you know his inmate number, because mail takes forever if you don't have the inmate number on the envelope."

Chris looked at me suspiciously. "Now, how would you know that?"

I glanced at my desk for a prolonged second. I could give a dozen different answers, but I decided truth prevails. Alden knew my story. Chris did not. "I've done time." He couldn't believe it, but he didn't show shock about my revelation either.

"Interesting," he said as he turned back to his work.

The next morning Chris walked into our shared office and said, "We need to talk." Google had given him thousands of internet searches about me and my story. He didn't seem skittish about it, but he boldly probed for more information. "If it was such a great plan, how'd ya get caught?"

"It might be a billion years before the stars aligned perfectly for an escape like ours, but the end of our ride rested mostly on my shoulders. I'm not a very good criminal."

Chris listened closely, "Go on."

"Don't get me wrong, John made some mistakes too. He took chances that he could have easily avoided. He didn't have to carry the popcorn for that lady at the movie theater. He could have stayed off the interstates like he insisted on the first day. We didn't really need to wait a week for a custom-painted tonneau cover. He could have simply worn the gray wig instead of that ridiculous rocker wig...

Chris sat patiently, fixed on my story.

I continued. "Perhaps more than all that, John wanted a normal life. He insisted on pushing the envelope. He wanted to go to the movies and eat fast food and have a good steak in a restaurant. He wanted to go sightseeing, all normal things that ultimately were recipes for capture. He didn't behave like a terrified fugitive from the law, he was too busy having fun.

A revelation dawned on me and bubbled to the surface where it found a voice. "Maybe he knew we would get caught and wanted to enjoy the only twelve days in his life worth living." I sat silently for a moment mulling over the circumstances.

Chris asked, "Okay, but again, how'd ya get caught?"

"Perhaps I led the feds to us when I sent the truck title to our hideaway. Okay. It was a really dumb idea, but I wanted to be legal." Chris didn't move. He just waited expectantly. "I sent the title for the truck to our getaway cabin in Tennessee. The fact is, the marshals would have never been sitting in the parking lot at Barnes & Noble when we walked by had I not dropped a bread crumb. Sure, I used an alias—Molly Rose—but I should have known better. Perhaps, underneath it all, I did know better but never wanted to admit it. It was my fault we got caught. I handed them our address."

Chris sat down and raised his next question, "How did it feel that day of the escape?"

"I was a nervous wreck; I was sure everyone knew something was up. But I think the only one who suspected anything was Brennon, my very first dog handler. He caught my eye, a puzzled look on his face. He glanced at the officer and raised a brow.

When they loaded that dog crate into the van, I just knew Brennon was going to sound an alarm, but he didn't. I climbed behind the wheel, waved to the officers as the gate opened, then drove off. As the others hustled back to their cells, eager to get out of the biting wind, Brennon stood with his hands in his pockets and watched me drive away.

Shaking my head, I continued, "Barely breathing, I waited for a siren to sound as I cleared the expanse between Gate Two and Gate One, but no one stopped me. I hissed at the dog crate, 'John, are you in there?' no answer."

Chris waited, "And then?" I enjoyed the cliff-hung expression on Chris's face. His attention and reaction made me want to share the full-blown drama. So, I obliged.

"After a few agonizing seconds, Gate One begrudgingly began to open in front of me. Driving forward to freedom, every moment seemed to be in ultra-slow motion. My heart pounded in my ears, even the blinking of my eyes felt like the slow roll of a prison door closing. The gravel road turned right, and my life turned with it. The road felt different from all the other days I'd driven it. But that day, there was no going back.

Chris continued to stare in silence, gripped by gravity.

"I didn't care about the price. If I'd known, I couldn't possibly have done anything different. Until that instant, it had all been a dazzling fantasy about running away with a handsome younger man, a 'bad-boy' who loved the way I smelled and talked. I turned onto the paved road of the city. The dog crate behind me remained still. Relieved at the silence, I began to picture myself at a dog adoption after all. My shoulders relaxed and I took a deep breath. I let myself believe for a moment that I had not thrown my life away.

Suddenly, an arm pushed through the side of the box from inside the crate and a manic laugh filled the van. I jumped. My body tensed and my heart raced. I yanked the wheel and slammed on the brakes. John said, 'Drive, Baby, drive' and I did."

Chris smiled broadly. Almost triumphantly. "Now that's a story."

\* \* \*

A month into my new life in Boston, Alden called me from downtown. He said, "I'm stuck in a meeting, and I just got a call from Chris. He was on his way to Maine to visit Oscar when he got pulled over; they've taken him to jail. He's going to be released, but he needs a ride. I need you to go to Peabody and pick him up."

"I can't. As terms of my parole, I can't have contact with anyone in a jail. If I go inside, I'll have to report it to my parole officers. I'm sorry. I can't do that."

"You don't have a choice. You work for me, and I need you to go. I'll call the jail and let them know that you are not coming in, but you will be there to pick him up in the parking lot."

Unamused, I made my way to Peabody.

*Alden didn't seem to care if I was putting myself at risk or not. Why couldn't I have just said no? A traffic stop—it's not like that's a felony. Maybe this won't be a problem.*

Anxiety and stress were finding me even here in Boston. It was impossible to run away from my problems. I was going to have to learn how to tackle them head-on.

I waited in the parking lot for forty-five minutes. I could stand it no longer. I went in.

An emotionless officer behind plexiglass asked, "ID?" I handed it over. Satisfied, they returned it to me. Chris came out with a grin on his face, a grin I didn't feel.

"My motorcycle is at a garage over in Gloucester. Let's go." Once in the truck, Chris explained, "A few years ago, one of Alden's workers fell off a window ledge and hurt his back. At the hospital they asked if it was work-related, and he said, yes. Then they asked who he worked for, and he said 'Chris Dorr,' which was technically true because I supervised construction. But legally, we all worked for Alden. My knowledge and experience with employment was nil and I trusted Alden. I trusted that he would not subject me to risk, especially risks that I didn't fully understand. I assumed that Alden would discuss with me the consequences of my participation in his work.

"Anyway, the Department of Industrial Accidents put out a warrant for me because they wanted me to appear in court and explain what happened. I had no idea until I got pulled over for an illegal lane change and they ran my license."

Chris retrieved his bike from the impound yard. He pulled up to a stop sign, turned his motorcycle off and walked back to the truck. "Toby, in case you lose sight of me, do you know the way back to the office?"

"I'll find my way."

Alden's willingness to force his hand tarnished my hopes for a perfect new life. Disillusioned as I watched Chris walk back to his motorcycle, I prayed for an answer.

*Oh, God this doesn't seem like such a great idea after all. Maybe I'm trapped here, too, in something not quite what I pictured. Why did you have me come to Boston? Why am I here?*

As Chris turned to wave at me, a clear answer from the same voice I'd heard that day on suicide watch filled the truck.

"He is why you're here. Chris is the reason. He needs you. You need him. You need each other."

## 29

# A Dagger with Two Edges

**I COULD NO LONGER SEE** Alden in the same rosy light. Alden had charmed me and my mom, but by forcing my hand, knowing that to do so would violate the conditions of my parole, Alden not only disrespected me, but had also used my disadvantage against me. My dream of a fresh start in Boston suddenly felt jeopardized.

Once revealed, Alden made no attempt to conceal his true character. He started with little things. He asked me to get some keys made at a local shop. When I returned with the new keys, Alden snatched one and left to try it on the lock. When I checked the keys left behind, I realized that Alden had the wrong one. I hurried to offer the correct key and found Alden filing on the edge of the wrong key. Annoyed, he said, "It doesn't work."

I offered the correct key and piped up, "It's the wrong key." He took the right key and the lock opened freely.

"Well now this key is ruined. You'll have to take it back and tell him he cut it wrong, and I need it replaced free of charge."

It took me but a fraction of a second to process Alden's command. I was shocked to think that a wealthy self-made guy would feel it necessary to take advantage of an old locksmith over a two-dollar key, and he asked me to lie to make it happen.

I said, "I'm not ripping off that sweet old guy."

Alden responded, "Well, I'm not paying for another key."

"Fine. I'll pay for it out of my pocket. I will not lie to him."

"Okay. You can pay for it." Stunned, I expected my offer would emphasize Alden's petty behavior, but instead, he took me up on it.

Such trivial stresses nibbled away at my makeshift peace, weakening my resolve. Alden centered my decision to rebuild in Boston; so much relied on our relationship; so much depended on a great launch into the unknown future. Already, I sensed the earth rumbling beneath my feet, drawing my attention from my new life to my old life, back to Greg's dilemma.

I'd left Kansas City and my son fighting for his life.

And yet, I felt compelled to report to work while my spirit grew darker. I stepped from the elevator into the large basement office space. I felt pressure from all angles: parole officers, Alden, Greg, Mom, my past, my future. A thousand emotions roiled within me.

Absolute physical confinement, a stark contrast to the incessant expectations that the world had imposed on me, dulled my sense of duty. Prison provided me a perfect alibi, some psychological justification to set aside my problems. While doing time, not only did nobody expect greatness, but contrarily, everyone expected failure, or perhaps worse. Strangely, I felt drawn to the freedom that prison bars provided. I began to see that it mattered not that I went to Boston, stayed in KC, or jumped borders to Canada. My problems would follow.

I began to cry.

I didn't recall where I landed that morning, but Chris overheard my sobs.

He stepped closer and asked, "What's wrong, Toby?"

At first, my troubles choked me. Chris somehow saw the clouds of demons in a frenzy around me. Waving his hands as if clearing the air, Chris said, "Let go of all those thoughts, Toby.

They aren't doing you, or your son, any good." The movement distracted me, and I took a moment to see Chris for the first time. Who was this person who seemed to have an insight into my very soul?

As it happened, the drama of the key scandal presented a perfect reflection of the toxic relationship that had developed between Chris and Alden.

The Department of Industrial Accidents enforced Worker's Compensation laws; they were the watchdogs over employers. Alden had hired a dozen illegal immigrants, mostly from the former Soviet country of Georgia. Alden paid them in cash, and when Chris came to work with Alden, Alden stopped paying the workers directly, preferring to provide Chris with cash that Chris would then dole out to the workers.

The worker's comp case shone the brightest spotlight on Alden's devious betrayal, and Chris suddenly found himself under the bus.

With a childlike trust and willingness, Chris shared with Alden an intimate, intertwined history. When recent events opened Chris's eyes to Alden's true nature, Chris blew the whistle—first with Alden's wife. When Chris advised her to run, Alden's response provided a clue to Alden's fear. The cards began to tumble, the first being Chris's credit card.

Until then, Chris had run Alden's construction projects sixteen hours a day. At the end of a year, they settled, canceling credit card receipts by the number of hours Chris worked, then paying the difference.

Cutting him off immediately left Chris penniless and homeless. Chris drove his motorcycle to an unheated camper on the south side of Boston. But, before Alden killed Chris's phone, I tracked him down.

When I found him, pouring rain had begun to freeze. "Get in the car, Chris. I'm taking you to dinner. Checkers insists."

At dinner, Chris relayed more of the story. "I have a lot of dirt on Alden. He's done unethical things, many of them criminal. I wanted to talk to the authorities about the worker's comp case and clear this up. Alden forbids me to talk. He threatened to cut me off financially, personally, and legally. Now, the State of Massachusetts holds a $60,000 judgment against me. Most of his construction projects are done so he doesn't need me anymore. I'm expendable. He was shocked that I said anything to his wife, and worried that I might say more. He knew I didn't have anywhere to go when he cut me loose. I gave him five years and all power over me. But now it's time to escape *my* prison."

"Glad to hear it. Next week is Thanksgiving, Chris. Come back to my apartment. I have an extra bed, and heat and laundry. I'll fix us a Thanksgiving dinner, and you can figure out what you're going to do. You'll think better if you're warm and dry. Plus, you can help me by walking Checkers."

Checkers won the argument and curled up on Chris's lap for the ride home.

In the car Chris asked, "Tell me more about John Manard."

Facing Chris while he drove through the night, I continued my story. "The day I met him, he walked boldly right up to me in the prison yard, unlike any other inmate. He stopped before me under a blazing sun. He offered his hand cordially, 'I'm Manard. I'd like to be your next handler.' I squinted one eye hard shut and shaded my other with my left hand. With my right, I took his and shook firmly.

"I had shaken a lot of inmates' hands, yet John was different. His silhouette seared my mind; for a shaving of a moment, I forgot to let go of his hand. Every bit of our first few seconds together transferred tons of chemistry. When I released his hand, he held his hand there in midair for a moment as if to offer a second chance, or perhaps to assert that he did not initiate the withdrawal. He intrigued me. When he spoke again, he jarred me awake, 'You need me in the program because I'm good, really good, probably the best dog handler in the prison.' I liked his confidence. I liked his swagger. I liked him."

When Chris and I returned to my apartment, Chris settled into my extra bed up in the loft. The next morning, I envied that Chris seemed to be free of Alden, while I went to work. I couldn't hide my feelings from Alden. I no longer trusted him, and he could tell.

One day, Alden stopped me and said, "I know this might sound cruel, but if you don't do as I ask, I'll have no choice but tell your parole officer that you've violated your parole and must be returned to prison. I don't want to do it, but I will. After all, you picked up Chris from the jail. That won't be a lie."

Alden planned to use my felony and my fear against me. Of course, Alden saw my vulnerability as someone he could control. Alden revealed a darker soul than anyone I'd ever met, including inmates. I wanted to run again, but the conditions of my parole bound me to Alden.

Alden took Chris's desk across from mine but never explained Chris's absence. In response, I used the wood stove on the other side of the basement as an excuse to take a different desk for the winter.

A week later, Alden finally said, "Toby, Chris isn't working here anymore. I don't know where he is. I've looked everywhere for him, even down at the trailer he has on that property his dad left him, but there's no sign of him. I'm assuming he went back to his mother's house in Maine. He doesn't have anywhere else to go. But if you see him hanging around, don't let him in, and call me. I need to know where he is and what he's up to."

I just nodded. I knew Chris's exact location, three floors above us in my apartment, but I didn't tell Alden.

One morning a local friend of Alden's came to visit, "I was just in the area and thought I'd stop in. I just passed Chris leaving the building walking a little black and white dog. How's he doing?"

Alden rudely ended the conversation as I braced for shock, "What is Chris doing in the building? I thought I made it clear, you are not to let him in."

"I haven't let him in the office. And I can have whomever I want in my apartment. We discussed that when I moved here. My apartment is a privately owned condo, not owned by you. My name is on the lease. You have no jurisdiction over my personal life."

"You don't know how dangerous Chris is. You don't know what he could do. He could take your keys while you're sleeping and come down here."

"If he wanted to take my keys and come down here, he could do it from wherever I lived."

"You take the day off and think about it. I need your answer tomorrow. Either Chris goes or you do. I'll fire you and report to your parole officers that you are unemployed which is a violation of your probation with the state of Massachusetts."

The time to act had come again, so I left the office and went to my apartment. Chris listened as I called my Kansas parole officers, starting with the fed.

"You can do your federal parole anywhere in the country, but you still have some time left on your state parole, and I think that might mean trouble. Let me know after you talk to your Kansas parole officer. But personally, I'd rather not see you anywhere near Alden. I knew there had to be something fishy with him pushing so hard for you to move there," my parole officer said.

The next call didn't go so smoothly.

"Toby, I'm sorry but there's no flexibility here. You were transferred to Massachusetts for that specific job. Without it, you can't be out of Kansas."

"I could find another job here."

"I could live with that, but the Massachusetts parole board won't. They weren't happy about taking you in the first place."

"It's only six weeks…"

"Doesn't matter. It could be one day, and the rules are the same."

"What are my options?"

"I can give you two weeks to get back here, but you have to come see me in person before the two weeks are over or you will be in violation."

Chris and I discussed options. I started, "Looks like I need to pack all this stuff up and follow the yellow brick road back to Kansas. What are you going to do?"

"I guess I could go to my mom's up in Maine."

"I'll drive you. I've always wanted to see Maine."

While Chris took Checkers for a walk, there was a knock on my door. Strange, because it's a secure building. It must be a tenant or perhaps Alden… I slowly opened the door to see my landlord, who coincidentally was a friend of Alden's.

"I just thought I'd stop in and see how you were doing. Alden tells me you're having some trouble."

She looked around the apartment as if she expected to see someone else there. "You know, you should be careful who shares your bed."

"There's nobody in my bed but my dog. I have two beds here. If I have an overnight guest, they have their own bed. Thanks for the advice. I haven't worked out the details yet, but it looks like I'll be going back to Kansas. I'll let you know when I figure out my plans. I know Alden prepaid for the apartment for a year. I'll sign a paper releasing the apartment back to you. Thanks for leasing it to me, I've loved it here."

"Take your time, you can stay here as long as you need to."

When Chris learned of the visit, he said, "That's no surprise, Alden's many resources double as spies. Don't worry, Toby. He

220

doesn't own you. It took decades for me to learn what you learned in only five months. Alden and I have been nearly brothers since I was nine years old."

I typed up my resignation letter and left it on Alden's desk in the middle of the night, along with my keys, laptop, and cell phone.

I needed to report to my parole officer by December 29.

Mother Nature delivered a winter doozy and Chris had a thought, "Toby, you don't know how bad storms get up here. I don't think you can drive a loaded truck for 1400 miles in a blizzard. I have no pressing demands; let's rent a car and beat the storm. We'll leave all your stuff here, check in with your parole people and then we'll drive back and get a U-Haul. I'll help you load it and then head for Maine."

Undaunted by my history, Chris's behavior revealed humility; without a shred of conflict, his profound acceptance inspired me to look through the pains of life to the beauty beyond.

Chris told me a bit more about his story, "I've traveled the world. First in the U.S. Navy and then as a contractor installing wet process stations. I spent Y2K in a bunker in Israel. I watched my biological dad beat my half-brothers into the hospital. My stepfather died of a drug overdose; my mother was a felon. And all three of them were great people.

"I fell overboard in the North Atlantic while commercial fishing. That should have been the end of me, but it wasn't. It took me twenty-four hours to warm up again. I dumped my motorcycle doing sixty miles an hour without a helmet on, and by the grace of God, I managed to miss the telephone pole. I spent four hours in a torture chamber interrogation room in a communist country. I watched thousands of bombs covered in personally vindictive sentiments launched into Kuwait and Iraq. I've even walked under my aircraft carrier when it was in dry dock. To fix the radar, I climbed the radio tower on my aircraft carrier during a typhoon in the South China Sea.

"I've been from one extreme to another. I was lost in the drug world for a year or so. I got baptized in an all-Black church in Harlem, New York. The only place I haven't been is prison. You've got me on that one.

"I've played the fool. I've been the victim, and I've stood up from ashes. Toby, your story doesn't scare me. There's nothing about your story that I find unredeemable. Through it all, wisdom, hard work, and words rule supreme."

I began to feel like home was next to Chris.

I accepted, "Sounds like a plan. We can have Christmas with my family. You'll love it!" Yet, the decision, earmarked by failure, felt more like a house of collapsed cards. So, with Checkers tucked between us, snow falling thick and heavy, and windshield wipers beating to classic rock, we headed for home, filling the miles with meaningful conversation.

My first Christmas back home felt awkward. One holiday dinner didn't bridge the chasm in our family. I missed the envelopes hung with care on inmate lockers.

When left alone, Mom asked, "Toby, I really like Chris. Is there something going on between you two?"

"No, Mom. He's just a good friend. We're both Alden's victims trying to find our way."

*Funny, through this entire journey, I never thought myself a victim, until now.*

I drew my shoulders up. "No, I take that back. We're not victims. We are more like two souls who've been thrust from darkness into the sunlight, and we are still rubbing our eyes and trying to make sense of it all. But I really wanted to make a new life in Boston. I loved it there."

"Well, I'm glad you're home. Boston was a great city and I know you could have done well there, but maybe you belong here."

Soon after, Mom offered Chris the basement.

The next day, Mom took Chris and me to see my brother's cottage. She said, "Now that I no longer have your Dad's income, my options are limited, so Anthony's going to fix this up for me to live in, and Tom and Susie are going to buy my place. I think I'll like a smaller space."

Chris looked around, calculating, and thinking. He looked at me, "I can do this work. I'll talk to your brother. You can help me, Toby. We can get this place ready for your mum in just a few weeks. Then we'll head back to Boston, there's no rush to get back there. I'll help you load your stuff and see you off."

The entire family breathed a sigh of relief with a viable plan to help Mom. At the end of the first week of working on Mom's new place, Chris approached me with another idea, "Toby, I need to start over too and Kansas City seems as good a place as any. How would you feel about renting a two-bedroom house; we could share expenses? Once we get on our feet, we can go our separate ways."

I responded, "I think we'd get further ahead if we didn't have to pay rent."

"I can't stay in your mother's basement. I need to move forward. I need my own place."

Chris felt squashed beneath Alden's thumb, and he stressed how urgent independence had become. Working together would ease the burden. To have someone to lean on and confide in would be welcomed. We'd gotten along well together over the last couple of months; I saw value in his suggestion.

"Okay, Chris. Let's do it," I agreed.

We finished the cottage and headed back to Boston, ending one chapter and starting another. Checkers came along for the ride to remind us that chasing balls with wind in our faces was nearly as great as second chances.

**30.**

## SONRISE

**BEFORE CHRISTMAS, GREG'S INSURANCE** required his first treatment to be a bone marrow transplant using his own bone marrow. How absurd! Modern medicine extracts bone marrow from a cancer patient, cleans it and replaces it. Could that even work? It made no sense, and it made no difference. Greg did not respond well.

I continued to honor Greg's wish to give him space. Mom kept me updated.

Greg's second transplant, scheduled for March, employed a more hopeful technique using his brother's marrow, a perfect match. However, each attempt meant Greg's entire immune system must be destroyed to ready his body for new marrow. In Greg's case, the cure was proving to be more damaging than the disease as the first transplant not only failed but sent Greg's health into a spiral. Prepping Greg for the second attempt shocked his body further, leaving him extremely vulnerable to infection. Greg had resigned himself to the idea that the fight was not worth it.

"Toby," Chris said over breakfast one morning, "I know you've been giving Greg his space, but you might think about going to visit him now. It seems like things are getting a bit desperate. Maybe he'd like his mom to be around."

I thought about it all week but hadn't decided, yet.

*Could I face another rejection? Maybe it is easier to just stay away.*

One day I had a meeting at church. As I left for home, I realized I was driving by Greg's hospital. Without a second thought, I stopped. Standing outside his room, fear kept me from pushing through the door. A nurse walked by. "Go on in. He can have visitors."

"Is anyone else in there?"

She poked her head through the door. "Nope. Greg, you have a visitor."

She turned to me. "Who are you?"

"I'm his mother."

"Greg, your mother's here to see you."

I took a deep breath and walked through the door, no turning back.

*Here is my son. Bald and beautiful. My strong, sensitive boy. Emily's gift. How did we get here?*

My mind registered Greg's proximity, but his eyes, his frozen, distant spirit made me feel a great magnetic force sloughing me as though the walls behind me were rapidly retreating, pulling me with them.

I held back my tears. "Greg, I love you. I always have."

"I know you do, Mom."

"How do you feel?"

"Tired."

"What does bone marrow look like?"

He laughed. "It's watery pink. Never thought I'd know what it looks like either."

The door opened. Rob walked in and stopped short when he saw me sitting there. His face turned to stone, and he tossed a bag on the empty bed next to the door. "Here's your stuff." And he turned and walked out.

"Rob, wait…" I called. The door closed.

I turned back to Greg. "Can I give you a hug?"

"No. You better go."

That night Mom called. "I hear you went to see Greg today."

"Yes, I did. He looks strong."

"Greg called his brother who called your sister who called me. He says it's too hard to see you. He wants you to stay away. He doesn't have the energy for family battles while he fights the cancer war. I'm sorry, Toby. I'm so sorry."

Gingerly I had hoped to heal our relationship, but accepted that the only thing I could offer Greg was love from a distance.

Ten days later, the phone rang again. "Toby," Mom said, "Greg is in a coma. His organs are shutting down."

Chris and I rushed to Mom's house, where she waited with one of my sisters.

With a sense of urgency, Chris said, "Toby, you and your mum need to go to Greg. There's no time to wait." My sister called ahead, warning others in my family at the hospital that I would be arriving soon.

Mom and I held hands as we walked into the ICU. A sister-in-law blocked the door. "This isn't a good time, Toby."

While my son lay dying beyond that door, my tolerance for my family's animosity struck an all-time low. I looked her straight in the eye and with a bit of sarcasm, I said, "No, it's not a good time, is it?" I put my hand on the door.

A brother-in-law came out. "You've picked a fine time to try and be a mother again, Toby."

"Oh. Will tomorrow be better? Because I don't think we have a tomorrow."

A team of doctors and nurses approached from down the hall. "Ms. Young, we're here to fulfill the wishes of our patient. He asked that you not be allowed in the room."

"Really? My son told you that if he was in a coma and his organs were shutting down, the most important thing he wanted you to do is keep his mother out of his room? I doubt it. Sounds more like something his father would say. I'm going in."

A staff member asked, "Well, could you wait over here in this consultation room while we figure things out?"

My mom sobbed hysterically. I had to hold her up. "How can they treat you like this, Toby? I don't understand."

How absurd that Greg's mother and grandmother were the only two people banned from his death bed. The entire debacle made me furious. My mom didn't deserve their vicious treatment. She had done nothing but love me. It was the same way she loved each of them, and yet they were weaponizing it against her.

Two policemen crowded into the consultation room. "We've been called to keep you out of your son's hospital room. If you don't comply, we may arrest you. What's going on here, Ms. Young?"

"My son is dying. I'd like to see him."

"Who has custody of him?"

"Nobody! He's almost twenty-five years old. Nobody has custody of him."

"Who raised him?"

"I did."

"Well, why are we here?"

"I have no idea. Bitterness, perhaps? You can ask the people in that room."

They left while I tried to comfort my mother. And I called my federal parole officer. "My son is in a coma and he's dying. My ex has called the police and is trying to keep me out of his room. The police have threatened to arrest me. I just want you to know what's going on."

"Toby, you get in that room and see your son. Nothing else matters. If you get arrested, I'll go to bat for you on this one. Go see your son. And keep me updated on how it plays out. Toby, I'm really, really sorry."

The police returned. "Ms. Young, we've gotten an agreement from your ex that you and your mother can come in for fifteen seconds. Not a minute—fifteen seconds. That's all. Oh yeah, and you're not to look at anyone else in the room because they don't want to see you."

"Oh," they added, pointing at Chris, "and he is not allowed."

As soon as Mom walked through the door she marched over to Rob and pointed her finger. "What is wrong with you? She. Is. His. MOTHER. What kind of monster are you?"

With my left hand, I pulled Mom closer. With my right I reached for Greg and leaned over him to whisper, "Greg, I'm here. I love you so much, and I am so very proud of you. You've fought a tough fight, but that's enough. Greg, it's okay to let go. Be at peace, my son." I kissed him, wrapped my arm around Mom, and we walked out of the room into the hallway where Chris put an arm around each of us as we made our way out.

My phone rang before we reached the elevator, I answered, "Hello?"

The voice at the other end simply said, "Greg is gone."

At home, I waited to be included in funeral decisions by a call that never came. I couldn't sleep. I paced the house at night, sobbing uncontrollably.

*How can a mother lose TWO children? God, you are asking too much of me. I barely survived the first one. How will I get through this?*

Greg left me questions without answers. Emily left me life without purpose.

Chris and I faced the uncertainties together, and with God, we grew to appreciate each other's gifts. Life had presented us many challenges and defeats, but together, we began to see the beauty beyond the pain.

As bad as I expected, funeral directors met me at the door to Greg's funeral, "Who are you?"

"His mother."

"Well, we have instructions…"

"I'm sure you do." I brushed past them.

Rob and Eric stood at the head of Greg's casket. My sister unwelcomed me to join them.

Mom grabbed my hand and said, "Come on Toby, we'll just make our own place." She led me to the foot of the casket.

*Oh, my poor boy. Just look at you. I think you would have hated all this makeup. Your class ring, that's a nice touch. Goodbye my sweet boy. I'll take it from here.*

I'd come to a new perspective on death and grief. Two of my children managed to quickly achieve God's purpose with a beauty unmatched. I missed them terribly but learned to be at peace.

Chris encouraged me to talk openly about them, which was the blessing I'd needed so long ago. I no longer kept my grief a secret any more than I kept my children a secret. It was better late than never.

I accepted that Emily left with little chance to show me her personality. With her, I buried my feelings. Greg helped me find those feelings.

Losing a child is never easy, and I found that losing an infant differed from losing an adult—an adult with opportunities to create and explore life. I kept Emily's passing a secret because I feared peoples' reactions. However, denial led to more denial, and nothing good came of it.

I learned that grief is neither good nor bad, it just is. What mattered was how I dealt with it.

My grief, like a physical wound, had festered within me since Emily's brief stay, preventing me from growing beyond her passing. I pretended to live in a perfect world; I honed my acting abilities for decades. However, had everything been perfect, surely John and I would not have escaped.

I watched, determined to honor Greg with my life, as the hearse carried him away. Part of me departed with him. I imagined lying there dead in a hearse. It felt eerily familiar, perhaps some cosmic reminder of my life with Rob, or my time on suicide watch.

How would I move on from this moment? I knew Chris would not let me keep this grief silent like I'd done when Emily died. And in some part, I was grateful for that.

# 31.

## LOVE STORIES

CHRIS AND I RETRIEVED MY THINGS from Boston and rented a little house in Overland Park. We lived on my divorce settlement, but relocating, exploring events in Boston, renting cars, eating, and ten thousand itty-bitty expenses dribbled us down to my last $5,000.

I gave it all to a man in Leavenworth about two miles from CCA; in return, Chris and I drove away with a 2005 red Dodge half-ton pickup truck. For the next five years, that truck represented the rudimentary lifestyle our lives would take, a perfect middle of the road between privileged rehearsal and John Manard, the meteor.

Between us, we could barely rub two pennies together, but Chris and I had a few good years of hard labor left in the tank; we welcomed risk, and God ran the show.

Chris sprung from a well of rich, worldly experiences. As deeply as he trusted God, he distrusted people. Life had hardened him, and I felt an opportunity to help Chris see humanity's value. For six months, we worked, ate, and slept, spending all twenty-four hours each day together. Our relationship had grown deeper before we realized that we'd become a couple. Naturally, Chris and I took the next step.

I showed him the money I made from eBay after I cleaned, photographed, posted, and shipped some old pottery. With the first few dollars, we began to browse local yard sales for more pottery. When it sold, we bought more. Chris washed and helped to photograph items, I photographed, posted, and kept the books. When we sold a piece, I printed the label, and Chris packed for shipping. Within a few months, Chris and I set a goal to spend $500 per month at yard sales. A half year later, we owned $20,000 in inventory and our house was stacked floor to ceiling. But our little rental house couldn't contain the growth.

Chris insisted that we needed a commercial property. I found a place for sale two hours east of Kansas City, so we looked. Chris felt supremely confident that he had the skills to rehabilitate the old building.

The city of Sedalia simply wanted someone to take it off their books.

Chris and I developed a use plan for the building and submitted a bid to buy it for $10,000 cash, the city's required minimum. Several weeks later, we received notice by mail.

Chris and I were the sole bidders on the severely disabled property. We won. However, we still had no money, not a dime. Sedalia set closing for two months later.

We scrambled to find help. When my aunt heard our story, she pledged to help us with half if we could find the other half.

Several days before the closing, my niece from the other side of the family had just cashed in her 401(k) to pay her debts and had $5,000 she could lend us.

On the day of the closing, we prayed that God would stand strong with us.

An attorney at closing opened the meeting. "We're sorry for the inconvenience but there is a small matter of closing cost that we need to resolve."

My heart sank, I asked, "How much?"

The attorney answered, "Sixty-three dollars."

Chris watched me write a check. I slid the personal check along with the cashier's check for $10,000 across the big oak table. We signed papers and left the title company in a dizzy haze. As we stepped outside, I checked on my phone the balance of our account. I showed Chris my phone, the screen glowed "$64.00." We closed with one dollar to spare.

God knew our troubles and solutions; He knew our strengths and weaknesses. God knew we needed each other, and Chris listened when God suggested that we make it official. Rather than a romantic gesture of love, Chris's proposal was more of a next logical step, but we were building and growing and healing.

Chris's mom welcomed me, "Marriage isn't two people facing each other and gazing lovingly into each other's eyes. Marriage is a journey. It's two people standing side by side and facing the same path together."

When the judge at the local courthouse asked me, I said, "I do." And Chris did too. I held a small bag with an outer netting of tatted beads that Lisa had made, and I wore a beaded tatted necklace from George.

As Chris and I grew closer he shared a piece of his story, "After my first marriage, I wasted thirteen years lamenting that I'd never find another wife, but my mom told me, 'Be patient, Chris. You don't know what God is putting her through to prepare her for you.'"

I laughed, "So, my going to prison was all YOUR fault then! Thanks a lot Chris."

Like an old cassette player with the fast forward button pressed down, 2009 squealed by at high speed. On Christmas Eve, while we sat up in bed late into the wee hours of the morning, we talked and laughed and rejoiced in our struggles. I turned to the nightstand next to the bed.

I remember thinking *I'd like some Chapstick*, but as I leaned toward the drawer, I blacked out.

Chris lifted me from the floor back to the bed. He shook me and asked, "Toby, are you okay?"

I tried to answer him, but something felt off.

Chris dialed his mom back in Maine for advice. His mom immediately thought, "STROKE!" Sixteen minutes later, Chris wheeled me through the door of the local hospital. My right side thrashed uncontrollably while my left flopped like an octopus on a sandy beach.

A medical team administered a stroke treatment that only works during onset. The results were remarkable. Chris, literally, and figuratively, saved my life.

Chris didn't coddle me when it came to recovery. The day I came home, a U-Haul took center stage, he said, "The best thing for a stroke is to get back on the horse."

He handed me a box, and we loaded the truck.

I walked away without visible effects. For several months, I struggled to find words and make decisions. Today, I only mention it when I need an excuse, like when I trip over a curb, "Ooops, sorry, I had a stroke, you know!"

My mother loved Chris from the moment she met him. They spent hours in deep contemplative conversation. And Chris loved my "mum" back, just as deeply. With an old, understanding soul, Chris reminded us of Dad, but like Emily and Greg, Dad had achieved his purpose, and Mom showed her age.

One day, Mom said, out of the blue, "Toby, you didn't cause your dad to die."

"What?"

"I'm sorry I ever said that."

"When did you say that, Mom?"

"In that *Wall Street Journal* article."

"Oh Mom, no apologies."

"Well, I just wanted to clear it up."

Twenty or more years had passed since Mom's diagnosis of COPD, but by then, cigarettes had exacted a heavy toll on Mom's health. It mattered not that she quit back then. Her condition worsened, starting with oxygen only at night, but progressing to a deep dependency that merely kept her alive.

With Mom growing frailer, I took her to the doctor. After her check-up, he asked me to a quiet consultation room, "Your mother has spots in her lungs, her health is declining rapidly. There's not a lot more we can do. Has she expressed her interest in knowing the details?"

I'm sure that my posture said enough, but to be certain, I shook my head. I followed him back to Mom's room.

I held her hand while the doctor spoke, "Mrs. Phalen, I just want to make sure we have your chart up to date." He scanned his clipboard and asked a series of questions, the last of which I knew was the real question, "Mrs. Phalen, would you prefer to be informed if we found anything more serious or life-threatening?"

Mom glanced at him then turned to the wall, with a dignified reservation in her tone, she said, "No, I don't want to know."

"Okay, Mrs. Phalen, I'll make a note in your chart. I've reviewed the results of your work. There's nothing of immediate concern. Call me if you need anything."

In the next few weeks, Mom's lungs filled with fluid. The doctors surgically drained them to help her breathe and then released her to rehab, but while there, doctors confirmed what we all knew: Mom was dying.

Chris and I visited on Sunday, the day before Mom would be released, to spend her last few days at home; we watched the Chiefs play, and Mom's spirits seemed high.

At halftime, an aide popped in, "Mrs. Phalen, I'm here to take you to respiratory therapy."

"You most certainly are not! I'm watching the Chiefs, and

tomorrow I'm going home to die. Do you know what that means? It means nobody can tell me what to do."

Chris smiled at her audacity.

I thought, *If only we could all be so bold.*

The next day, hospice delivered a special bed and supplies to Mom's cottage. I presented Mom with the two obvious options, "What do you think, Mom? Would you like the privacy of your own bedroom, or would you prefer your bed in the day room where you can see your garden and bird feeders?"

"Well, I'd like the garden view."

The next day, two of Mom's many grandkids came on horseback to Mom's door.

"Open the doors!" Mom commanded with a rasp. Through the French doors, Bertie the horse clopped her front hooves and the girls giggled to their grandmother. The sand of Mom's hourglass ran short, and sunshine, children, horses, laughter and love were never more precious.

The hospice nurse carefully checked a long list of bed adjustments, medication doses, item positions on shelves, electronic entertainment, and countless other details to make Mom comfortable. Then the nurse met with us in the kitchen to instruct us and explain what to expect.

We solemnly filed out of Mom's cottage, but Mom singled me out, "Toby, stay here."

I took her delicate hand and asked, "What do you need Mom?"

"You're the only one who will give me the truth. What did that nurse say in your meeting?"

"She told us that it's normal for you to see people that we can't. She told us to be brave. You know, Mom, I really wish I could see them too."

Many decades had silvered Mom's hair and wrinkled her face, but her eyes still shone like they did the day Dad appeared at the top of the basement stairs. "How much time do I have?"

"Well, we don't know." I began to explain, "There are a lot…"

Mom waved her hand, cutting my words as they left my mouth. She never stood for sugar-coated stories, and nothing had changed, "I know she gave you an idea. Tell me."

"Ten days, Mom. She said it could be ten days."

Mom looked out her window and then glanced around her room, taking in all her favorite things filling the walls. Then she looked back at me. "Okay. Toby, I can do that. I'll give you ten days, but not a single day more."

Her eyes moved to the book on her nightstand. "I'll never know how my story ends."

"Would you like me to read it to you, Mom?"

I read to her every chance I could get. I read in the middle of the night, I read in the mornings, I read after dinner. I read to her, perhaps, more importantly, I read *for* her. The only thing left I could give her, I read while she slept and sometimes I'd hear her whisper some acknowledgement, some statement like, "Don't do it. It's a trap." And I knew she heard me.

As her days grew shorter, so did my tolerance for book details that didn't matter, so I skimmed to the good parts with perseverance to complete the book before Mom's time had come.

Mom did see people I couldn't see. Just outside those French doors where the horse had made its visit, Dad and Father Davern waited. I longed to hear her mention Greg or Emily, but she never did.

One night I noticed her twisting the blanket in her lap. "Mom, is somebody here? Are you wrapping someone up in your blanket?"

She whispered sweetly, "Yes, it's Baby Jesus."

On the tenth day, exactly as she promised, Mom left us. I gave the eulogy at her funeral, "My mother was the strongest woman I ever knew…"

**She still is.**

## 32

## FULL CIRCLE

**SEVERAL YEARS INTO OUR MARRIAGE,** I received a phone call from a reporter. "Toby, this is Allen. I talked to you a couple of years ago."

"Yes, I remember."

"Well, I've been talking to John Manard for a few months. He asked me to give him your phone number. I didn't want to do so without your permission."

Listening to the call, Chris spoke up. "Toby, give him your number. You must talk to him. John needs a friend, and you need closure."

A week later, my phone rang. The digitized recording stated coldly, "This is a call from New Hampshire State Prison. Press one to accept the charges from…" After a slight pause, John's recorded voice said, "John Manard."

I looked at Chris; Chris nodded reassuringly. I pressed the button.

For an eternal moment in my heart, I felt teleported back to that night in Tennessee when they took John. I imagined pressure in my back like that of an officer's knee making it difficult to breathe, I remembered the ache I felt to tell him "Goodbye." The phone clicked, I stared at Chris whose face remained calm and assertive. My voice trembled…

"John?"

"Toby, how are you?" John's deep, smooth voice cradled me carefully. Chris's eyes reflected strength, character, and confidence, a safe place to run to.

To prepare for that call from John, Chris and I talked about it. Chris deeply knew that John posed no threat, and I knew I no longer needed to run. So Chris scrunched his eyes closed for a long second while nodding, like a father might reassure a little one who's trying again to ride a bike, then he stood and walked to the kitchen. I walked to the window, "I'm well, John. How are you?" Tears filled my eyes, and my voice broke more, but my heart remained strong.

I cried for John; I cried for us. But as we talked, I felt relief that my future and self-esteem no longer flowed from John. John and I would forever remember how twelve days changed our lives, but our lives couldn't be more different. Chris was right. John needed a friend and I needed closure to the fantasy.

John called several more times, Chris introduced himself. With love and laughter, Chris established boundaries, while John and I started to fill in the gaps of what happened since our arrests.

Without much compassion, prisons often trade unwanted troublemakers. One such trade took John to New England, not far from Chris' hometown, so when Chris and I planned a trip, John urged us to apply for a visit pass.

"John, nobody is going to let me visit you in prison. I helped you escape!"

"You never know, Toby. Just fill out the papers and see what happens."

Chris and I were approved.

I had transitioned through prison gates dozens of times, but never as a visitor to an inmate. Procedures dehumanized, demeaned, and scrutinized us. In visiting John, I discovered yet even deeper appreciation for the sacrifices Mom made for me.

A correctional officer directed Chris and me to seats at a table in a well-lit room filled with other tables. John appeared from a door at the rear of the room. With a smile and signature swagger, he approached and took a seat.

Chris and I smiled too. Chris said, "Wow! At last!"

Through all the muck of prison life, I sensed John's spirit glowing. He looked at me, "Toby, how are you, girl?" Then he looked Chris in the eye and cordially said, "Welcome to New Hampshire." John's words again, audaciously implied that he somehow owned the state of New Hampshire and that he alone held the authority to welcome us.

The moment hung precariously, like a joke waiting for the punchline. I had facilitated the escape of a convicted murderer, took a conviction in the process, then sat there in a New Hampshire State Prison laughing with the very same John Manard.

Chris asked, "Do you suppose they know what's going on here?"

John smiled, "Chris, you know the prison system couldn't track a fox at a fish fry!"

Years of curious questions had lingered. John and I shared prison stories and laughed and reminisced, but the truest satisfaction came not with our conversation but with our rendezvous. Meeting John liberated Chris and me more profoundly than ever.

"I was really worried about you, Toby. You're not prison material, and it just broke my heart to think of you behind bars. I know I told you they wouldn't sentence you, but I forgot about Martha Stewart. They do send important people to prison. I'm really sorry."

"John, I'm sorry that you got all this extra time added to your sentence. Another ten years..."

"No, Toby, I got twenty."

"Twenty? How'd that happen?"

"Your sentences ran concurrently and mine should have, but the federal prosecutor found a way to make mine consecutive. I know she tried for a deviation on your sentences, but I'm glad the judge saw the kind of person you are and denied it."

"How did you know that?"

"Toby, I knew everything you were going through. I have my ways. I kept track." John had proven that he did have ways to obtain information, but John was also an inmate with an ego who projected super-human abilities that I sometimes questioned.

"Your life is ruined, John. You'll never get out. I'm so sorry."

"I ruined my life before the escape; I was never getting out anyway. You gave me twelve days to be a real human being, twelve precious days worth a lifetime. I have no regrets."

"Manard, time's up." The officer called from his desk.

"If I'd had more notice, I could have set up a day long visit for us, Toby."

Chris shook John's hand. "I'm glad to have finally met you in person. I've heard so much about you and now I see it was all true. You're a good guy, John. I'm sorry you're here. We'll help you in any way we can to make your prison stay more bearable."

"I like you, too, Chris, and I don't like many people. I'm glad Toby has you. Take care of her."

We started to leave but I turned back. Hugging him once more, long, and hard, I said, "Goodbye John," and then, holding Chris's hand, I walked away without looking back.

Our visit symbolized the conclusion I needed. Chris and I faced a clean future.

# 33.

## STRONGER BROKEN

YEARS FLEW BY; CHRIS AND I created new lives together. The keel to my boat in stormy seas, Chris keeps me steady and on course. Providing him the home and stability he had been searching for his whole life, I am Chris's anchor. Together, we are unsinkable.

Chris restored bricks and timber while I focused on building a web design business. We leveraged our best past skills and remained excited about the future. We often walked to Subway for breakfast, where one morning a newspaper left on a table caught my attention.

I took Chris's hand and said, "Let's walk." As we meandered toward home I asked, "Did you see today's paper?"

"No. What's up?"

I held up the headlines, "New York prison worker, Joyce Mitchell, charged with helping inmates escape."

Chris's eyes narrowed like lasers acquiring a target, and I knew he took me seriously.

I continued, "The inmates are on the run, each convicted of murder. They say she loved one of them. The media's gonna come calling. They'll wanna know why. Should I talk? Can I offer hope to that poor woman in New York? At this point is silence even an option?"

"You're not invisible, Toby."

"So, I talk?"

"It's up to you, but that's my vote."

Come they did, in droves. *Dateline, The Atlantic Magazine*, the BBC, *Anderson Cooper, Inside Edition*, Brooke Baldwin, *The New York Post, The Kansas City Star*, even a news crew from Japan solicited my thoughts. I began to see that women everywhere needed hope that perhaps only I could inspire. I wanted the world to know that we are better than our worst mistakes.

I found inspiration nine years earlier, and Joyce Mitchell's story inspired me yet again to find my voice. The time had come to act on the promise I made while on suicide watch.

John looked beyond my cloak of invisibility. I found it easy to love someone who so deeply craved my offering. I'd come far to understand that neither the world nor my family controlled my self-worth. I learned that I had no power over other peoples' perceptions and only I controlled mine. I'd come to see that loving another was a gift to me that required no reciprocation.

When Dad chased that elusive white picket fence by moving our family half a dozen times, he ached for the carefree days of kites flying, towering castles surrounded by vegetable gardens, and giggling children, but he feared the shadow of that weeping willow. Dad's physical injuries healed with scars, but beyond his skin, as beautiful and powerful and honorable as he was, Dad carried emotional injuries that persisted in the shadow of fear.

In high school, as a gift, I wrote a heartwarming tribute to my dad for Father's Day. I watched his eyes carefully as he scanned the opening phrase, "During the month of May, 1963..." Dad's face drained of color as he abandoned my gift to Mom, "Here, Peg. We'll save this for later."

His message was loud and clear. Incapable of the conversation, perhaps had he seen what I saw... "each scar, a badge of courage, each step, a step of joy, each tear, a declaration of love. This was my greatest gift ever, one I always treasured and one that can never be equaled: a gift of love, suffering, strength, and joy called *Dad*."

Dad's behavior nurtured a code obeyed by our whole family, a code of silent tolerance. Yet, deeper still, I learned from him to use silence as a coping mechanism.

A decade had passed since John Manard asked, "Why do you stay married to him?"

Finally, God had given me the eyes to see how fear prevented joy. The thought of leaving Rob had terrified me.

John's eyes, his hands, his words, melted my fear. I loved him. Love gave me the courage to change and the desire to no longer accept anything less. Love won.

I found that to grow and heal, I had to walk away from some of the people I love most dearly. Forgiveness is a powerful thing. Even when it seems the behavior of others is more than you can bear, forgive anyway. Forgiveness is the greatest expression of love. It took me a decade before I could truly forgive those who tried to hold me back.

In learning to give voice and space to Greg's death, I also freed myself from the unresolved grief of Emily's death. Greg had such a dry sense of humor and was the world's best practical joker. Just saying his name brings a smile to my face.

I never knew who Emily might have been, but I know that for eighteen hours and thirty-one minutes, she was mine and I've come to accept that as enough.

My path has yet to intersect again with my oldest son.

Many years of sweeping out the cobwebs of my mind had passed since the day that I received notice of my release date from prison. I felt a similar emotion upon the news of a release date for this book. Who else would I call but George, of course!

She had lived this story by my side, yet George's words expressed my heart, "We stood up beneath the weight of the world. We rejoiced, and we cried, yet, together, we are forever changed."

Perhaps a dramatic prison escape bottoms the list of most elegant change methods, but had I chosen more wisely, I could not have learned more. God's power was made perfect in my weakness. The character I found in the darkest valleys pushed me to grow and become more. The best journeys were the most difficult and molded me into a strong woman.

Resist fear. Love with your whole heart. And live your life with conviction.

# EPILOGUE

**THE RELATIONSHIPS I BUILT** with women in prison were deeper and more profound than any other friendships I've had.

Both Jessica and her mother wrote to me. Jessica wanted to tell me Angie took my place and was watching out for her. Jessica's mother thanked me for being such a good friend to her daughter and told me that no one else had ever stood up for Jessica and neither of them would ever forget me.

Carly and I are still in touch. I sent her some pajamas when she moved back to minimum custody and could wear street clothes. Carly has been out of prison for several years, but her mom died before Carly's release. I never made it to Wichita to visit her, but I did save a card she wrote to me:

> *I just re-read the garden book we found that day in the library and thought of you and the book you made me. I found a picture of mint and a squash flower. Thought you'd get a kick out of them, though they're not nearly as cute as what you put in my book.*
>
> *I had a dream about you last week. I came to your place when I got released from here, but you had*

*no idea who I was. In the dream you were nice enough to offer me supper but when you brought it to the table it was a RAT—still had hair and eyes opened and it was a light tan color, looking right at me. Some friend you turned out to be! Figures.*

*All my love.*

*P.S. I sent the book you made home with my mom a couple of years ago. She's passed away since then, so I'm not sure what finally happened to it.*

*Carly*

Faith was one of the few women I knew who took her case to trial. For the inconvenience of that, the feds gave her an extra-long sentence. We corresponded while she was in prison, but I lost track of her when she was released.

Her first year in prison, Faith asked if I would order a special birthday gift for her daughter. I did order and pay for it. Faith had a tough road, but she walked it with dignity... and faith.

Reggie and I wrote throughout the rest of her sentence. She and I lived in the same town after her release, and we got together. I took her to breakfast a couple of times and Reggie helped us during one of our many moves, loading those darn U-Hauls. Reggie drifts in and out of her addiction. I'm always here for her when she needs me, but I won't enable her. She knows I love her.

George is my soul sister. After her release, she took in a dozen different teenagers whose parents were in prison. It all started with her daughter's classmate who was sleeping in a window well and washing in a public bathroom. Today that boy, her first foster son, is a registered nurse.

George refused to go through the foster care system because she didn't want to get paid for doing God's work. Instead, she worked with her federal judge who began referring teens to her. George officially adopted one of her foster teens and two of them still live in her house as young adults finishing college. All but one of her fostered teens stay in touch with her regularly.

George's cancer has returned, and she's accepted that there's little to be done. I spend several hours with George each week, walking when she can, but mostly just sitting together and talking. There's no one else I can relate to better because few have shared our journey.

For years, I wrote and talked to Lisa regularly. Chris even spoke with her by phone.

Even during her sentencing, Lisa's first concerns were for those of us who loved her.

Excerpts from her letters:

> *I miss you so much. It's not the same with you and George gone.*

> *April 4th, this Friday, I will go to court to be sentenced. I'm okay—everyone worries. Remember what I have said—my life is in God's hands and no other. Whatever happens, remember that. No crying. I have a lot to look forward to.*

> *Love ya,*

> *Lisa*

---

> *We moved this past week, and I found your Valentine's card I made so I'm enclosing it in here.*

*My attorney is coming next week to discuss my appeal. Will let you know how that goes.*

*Better go for now. I miss you, my friend. Say Hi to George for me.*

*-Lisa*

————————————

*Dear Toby,*

*Sorry I missed your birthday, I don't usually forget, but a lot of stuff here going on.*

*I'm sure you are wondering where I am in the appeals process. I'm at the 2255 stage where we have to prove my attorney was incompetent. The attorneys I have don't tell me much and there are endless delays. But, if we are granted hearings, I will come to KC and I hope you will be able to come see me.*

*So, I have some good news too—this warden gave me email! I don't think you had it. But if you want to do this, I would love staying in touch with you. I miss you so much my friend.*

*Love you lots,*

*Lisa*

Lisa and her husband sent me a card when Greg died. But somehow, as time moved on, the stretch between our letters got longer.

And then came January 13, 2021, but that's a story of its own.

# Becoming Free

the future looms
along the horizon
distant still yet
just out of reach

months to contemplate
knowledge to wisdom
quiet acceptance to courage
yearning to peace

the future belongs
to my becoming

unraveling layers,
decades worth of
ignoring, pretending,
settling for just enough.

the future blossoms with
righteousness and glory
no longer settling
but instead reaching out

knowing.
accepting.
forgiving

becoming
free

Written by Toby while at Houston Federal Prison, April 2008

# ACKNOWLEDGEMENTS

**MY FRIEND STEVE WROTE TO ME** every single day while I was in prison. Every. Single. Day. That's dedication and friendship. He never got tired or wavered in his support of me. Besides the letters, his monthly phone bills equaled a car payment, yet he never told me to stop calling.

The Toby Tribe—friends of my parents, friends from work, friends from groups I had belonged to, teachers I'd had. These angels showed up at all my court dates, donated books, wrote letters of support to my judge, and kept me in their thoughts and prayers.

To the women I've never met who continue to encourage me to speak out because I was "telling their story too." I hear you Sisters—March On!

My writing family encouraged me through this telling, Wendy, Leslie, Marilynn, Lisa, Kathryn, Kristin, Kitty, Diane, Simona, Sara, Katie, and so many more. You have my heart.

Special shout out to Lexi, Michelle, Karen, Tascha, and the GracePoint Publishing team who believed in my story, maybe even more than I did. You helped me find my voice.

Special thanks to my brothers: Tom for always being there for me and loving me steadfastly; I would have been lost without you.

And Jim, who always took charge of the details.

To my sisters. I love you and I miss you all so very much. But I must be me.

To Emily, you are never forgotten.

And to Greg, love echoes in the space you left behind.

Andy, I love you. Be free.

To Kevin and Lucia who opened their arms, hearts, and home and gave me a family. I love you both.

To Mom, I know I wouldn't be here today without your unconditional love. I feel you holding my hand. You remain the strongest woman I've ever known.

To Dad, you gave me wings. Your belief in me has been the wind that carried me through some turbulent storms. I still work hard to make you proud.

Last, but certainly not least, my Husbadorr who encouraged me to keep pulling off those scabs and digging at those old, poorly healed wounds. Ahhhh, the many, many tears it took to blossom. God has the best plans, doesn't He?

she is my favorite visitor
the light at the end of my week
I know she will make me smile
and wash away the bleak

she's the song my heart sings,
the smile and hand on the glass
she makes me believe in myself,
that this, too, shall pass

buoyed by the strength and faith
which only a mother's love brings
I can heal the broken me and fly
away on my father's wings

Written by Toby while at CCA, December 2007

# THE UNLEASHED SERIES

**I KNEW THAT TELLING MY STORY** could change the lives of women, but during a Women Starting Movements Conference in Chicago, I realized that many of the women I wanted to reach may not have the personal tools they need to change their lives. On the train ride home, I drafted a plan for a series of workbooks that could walk women through the journey of transformation.

The Unleashed Series programs provide a roadmap to redemption, helping women escape their prisons and rebuild their lives. Introducing powerful character traits such as gratitude, courage, respect, compassion, and faith, these workbooks focus on laying a foundation on which to build a purposeful life.

Starting with a journey of transformation, women learn the value of being part of a healthy community and are introduced to loftier principles such as the value of having a vision and discovering their unique passions while exploring ways to bring them forth.

Making a difference across the country, The Unleashed Series reaches women from many walks of life.

Our newest addition of a leadership series expands our mission.

Escape your prison today at TheUnleashedSeries.com
We'll be waiting...

# READER'S GUIDE

THE FOLLOWING CONTEMPLATIONS are for use in a book club or to spark conversations with your friends and community. They can also be used for personal reflection. I hope what you find brings insight and clarity to your world.

1. Shame creeps into our lives. Describe your Shame Dragon.

2. How would your mom describe your strengths? Those are your sword words against your Shame Dragon.

3. Victim or Victor? You choose. (Hint: you can choose only one.) Describe the difference.

4. What happened as a child? What did you lose or learn from it?

5. Focus on the beautiful lining in your grief. And, let go.

6. Describe your journey to redemption.

7. Who offended you? Are you on that list? What are you going to do about it?

8. Forgive. It does a body good. (Remember, to err is human; to forgive, divine)

9. Escape your prison, not your story. What's your story?

10. What falls have you taken in your life? (I must say, pedestals are overrated.)

11. To love another, love yourself. Write yourself a love letter and expect the best.

I'm just curious, how far would you go to escape your prison?

## ABOUT THE AUTHOR

**HAVING NEVER HAD** so much as a traffic ticket, Toby Dorr shattered her mold of perfection by helping a convicted murderer, a trainer in her prison dog program, escape in a dog crate.

Her story is a lesson in perspective. Instead of focusing on everything she lost, Dorr made a conscious choice to use her twenty-seven months in prison as a period to reflect on her life, heal emotional wounds, plot a course for the future, and embrace the sisterhood of women she encountered behind bars.

Far from easy, her prison sentence was gut-wrenching and devastating. But a pivoting revelation during a stay in suicide watch gave her purpose and direction. Filled with drama, action, adventure, heartache, and redemption, Dorr bares her soul and tells a story of heartbreak, courage, grace, and transformation.

While the escape made national headlines and captured the imaginations of an entire country, Dorr's memoir is an inspirational invitation to look upon life with self-acceptance and love. She pushes readers to move beyond the confines of their circumstances and live each moment with conviction, allowing its fullest, most beautiful potential to unfold.

To find out more, scan the QR code to visit Toby's website.

For more great Empower Press books visit
Books.GracePointPublishing.com

If you enjoyed reading *Living with Conviction* and purchased it through an online retailer, please return to the site and write a review to help others find this book.

CPSIA information can be obtained
at www.ICGtesting.com
Printed in the USA
JSHW010335161022
31628JS00002B/8